The Facts of Love

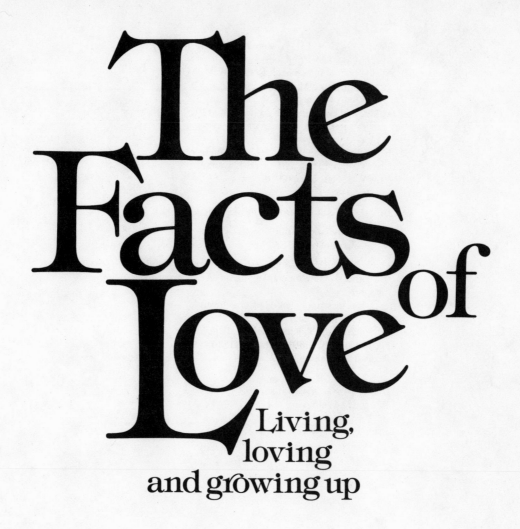

The Facts of Love

Living, loving and growing up

**ALEX COMFORT, M.D.
& JANE COMFORT**

Illustrated by Howard Pemberton and Bill Prosser

Crown Publishers, Inc.
New York

THE FACTS OF LOVE was edited and designed by
Mitchell Beazley Publishers Limited,
87-89 Shaftesbury Avenue, London W1V 7AD.
Art Editor: Anne-Marie Hughes

First published in the United States of America by
Crown Publishers, Inc., One Park Avenue,
New York, New York 10016.

Library of Congress Cataloging in Publication Data

Comfort, Alexander, 1920 —
    The facts of love.

    SUMMARY: Presents factual sex instruction and
the authors' advice for conduct based on concern
for others.
    1. Sex instruction for children — Juvenile
literature. [1. Sex instruction for youth]
I. Comfort, Jane T., joint author. II. Title.
HQ53.C65 1979 301.41'07 79-11520
ISBN 0-517-53839-3

Photoset in Great Britain by
Pierson LeVesley Limited

Printed in the United States of America

Can that be Love that drinks another
as a sponge drinks water?

WILLIAM BLAKE

PREFACE FOR PARENTS

Although this is a book for children, it should really be dedicated to parents. It is anxious work raising children in a world where norms of behavior in all areas—not only sexual—are in flux. But sexual problems bulk very large: daughters in particular at 12 or 13 may face situations which would faze a woman of 30. The "sexual revolution" has moreover spilled into (or been promoted by) the media, and prompts constant questions, often about matters which adults find difficult to discuss. Inputs from parents are diluted. They know that whatever *they* tell their children, others will be telling them something quite different.

Our book is meant for parents to give to children, from the age of, say, 11 upwards. Children differ at any given age in the information they need and in their reading skills—there is no age, however, at which this book would be *in*appropriate: younger children will probably skim through it, coming back for more specific information as they get older.

People who themselves enjoy and value sexuality, as well as those who (like most of us) have sometimes found it stressful or anxious, will recognize if they look candidly at their own growing-up experience, that they wish they had known more, not less about it: that they had been able to ask questions and have them answered. They will also recognize the immense difficulty, when one is adolescent, of really understanding experiences and emotions one has not yet had. In any other area from football to finance, open conversation with adults is a way of acquiring worldly wisdom—but not here. *Most* parents find it extremely hard to talk to children about sex— either in general or, still more, in terms of their own experience.

All parents want to protect their children from needless risks without preventing them from becoming responsible and enjoying adults. Most parents have some moral positions they would be unhappy to see their children abandon—whether these are religious insights, ordinary consideration for others, or simply wise and prudent behavior. It is up to each of us to speak for the principles by which we live, and commend them to others—particularly our children.

The authors of this book are no exception. What we say is, naturally, what we ourselves believe. Although most of what we have written here comes under the head of factual information, we have taken a very firm line concerning two kinds of behavior—reckless production of an unwanted child, and selfish and inconsiderate sexual behavior generally. In both cases the reason for the advice is concern for others as a basis of conduct. This would be understood and approved by most youngsters at any age. Some parents, we know, will wish to communicate to children their condemnation or approval of other kinds of behavior, or specific religious principles, but there would be general agreement, we think, over these two concerns at least.

One hears it said less often than in the past, though it still *is* sometimes said, whenever a school board tries to introduce a sex instruction syllabus, that "sexual knowledge is a beautiful secret, which should only be entrusted to children when they need it and are ready for it." Even if this were true (which depends on how we view the needs of children) such an argument today borders on self-deception. Citizen groups have sometimes grudgingly allowed sex education in schools with the proviso that thorny subjects (abortion, homosexuality, masturbation, birth control) are banned. Aside from the fact that these are among the subjects about which youngsters experience most anxiety, all the major newspapers, magazines and networks discuss them, often explicitly and at length. Faced with this barrage of half-understood and rather scary information any child able to read could be said to need and be ready for a factual explanation of what all that is about. Moreover one American girl in ten now becomes pregnant in her teens, and one in 20 before completing school. It looks as if the "beautiful secret" is simply no longer classified.

In states which allow it, there is school sex education. Many parents, by no means bigots of any stripe, feel strongly that teaching their children about morally important subjects such as sexuality is something they do not want to delegate to schools, because they want to check on what is being taught. That feeling is absolutely reasonable. Some schools check out sex-education materials with parents. Nearly all permit opting out. But in that event the parents must give comprehensive instruction themselves. Faced with the curiosity of their children and the fact that talking about sex is bound to raise questions about their own sex lives, if only by implication, it is absolutely normal for the best of parents to experience embarrassment, to run short of answers, or to be struck dumb. The more responsible they are, the harder it is to tackle such explosive subjects with confidence.

Preadolescent children, moreover, although they love facts, have great difficulty in understanding what any part of adult sexuality is about: they find it physically odd, factually intriguing, and emotionally unintelligible. Adolescents experience for the first time the force of sexual drives. They have great curiosity about putting them into practice, and also much anxiety about the changes in themselves. They worry about feelings they do not understand, have doubts about their own worthiness and attractiveness, and find it hard to set limits for themselves. They also find it hard to talk, and worry about how their parents will react. This mixture adds up to accident-proneness: the accidents range from inadvertent pregnancy and compulsive promiscuity on the one hand to disabling shyness, numbness and guilt which can permanently handicap personal relationships on the other. It seems that parents in general have had a raw deal from "experts" in the matter of child rearing. Successive faddists have presented them with "authoritative" but opposite advice. Parents who defend their own traditional values have often seen experts stoking up a climate in society hostile to those values. Worst of all, the parent has been a general scapegoat for any problems encountered, or excesses committed, by children, from drug addiction and dropping-out to mental illness. Experts, moreover, are puncture-proof. When their confident advice turns out to be silly, disastrous in application, or just simply wrong, they change tune with unruffled confidence and no blushes. Probably the best test of advice is whether it is also common sense. At the same time, knowledge is important, if only to get the facts right. But the perplexed parent who mistrusts school sex education (because education in general isn't delivering, and parents would like a say in what is taught, and how), doesn't want to leave it to experts (who may be kooks), and doesn't feel confident in handling the area himself, or herself, needs assistance, not blame. Some parents are really quite scared of their children. Next to man-eating sharks, kids who are possessed by devils are becoming the most popular characters in fiction and movies. We forget that we probably scared *our* parents at times, though nothing like as much.

We do have to talk to our children about sex. When parents try to do this, and look for help from books, they will obviously want to use those books which will give their children the kind of sex education which they, the parents, approve—not the kind which strangers who wrote the books might happen to prefer. Now there is no way a book on sexuality can be written with which every one of us will agree. In a good parent–child relationship, however, books are not handed out as authorities, but rather to set the ground for talking. The main use of adult books which we have written on sexual behavior has been to help spouses talk to one another about needs, feelings, and sexuality generally without being embarrassed. A book for children has the same use—to the extent that it can help them talk to you and you to them; in the course of doing this, you can establish where you disagree with what we say. You may disagree very strongly indeed, on specific points, or with our attitude in general, but the very presence of a statement in a book which you and your children read and discuss together introduces children to ideas they will in any case hear elsewhere. Books enable you to confront these questions in a setting where you have the chance to say what you personally think about them, and why. They are means of communication, not unchallengable authorities.

We cannot repeat too often that the key to the operation is with parents, not book authors. If you as parents think our emphasis is mistaken, if you have strong contrary views you want your children to heed, if our advice differs from your life experience (we come down hard on alcohol, while you may think social drinking is a necessary skill, for example), communication and discussion should be opened when you tell your children so. The ease with which this happens will depend on many things. Our object is simply to make it easier in general.

Sex education has often been accused of exciting youngsters and setting sex in motion ahead of time. Youngsters are now often set in motion ahead of time, but by the general behavior and attitude of society, not by sex education. Children growing up in modern America will "want to have sex" without prompting from us. The accidents which occur are not usually the result of knowledge, but rather of insufficient knowledge and not meeting with frankness from adults which might have prepared them for experiences they did not anticipate. Pregnancy and venereal disease, in particular, though they are not always prevented by knowing the facts, are promoted by *not* knowing them. Few people would now openly admit that they hope to keep babies and syphilis as judgments on vice. So sex education has to be given *before* it is needed for practical purposes.

We have tried to make this a multilevel book. The age at which children can read it will be determined, in America, chiefly by reading skills. Younger children will look at the pictures and skip in reading the text; it is designed so that they can return to it later. They may also go to you, their parents, with questions. It is valuable to know that the facts are there when they are wanted.

But why ahead of time? Why before they are actually involved when they may not be interested, or understand what they read, or what you say?

The answer is that lack of timely parenting in sexual wisdom has stopped being a deficiency and has become an emergency. Pregnancy is epidemic not just in the obviously nubile but in 15-, 14-, and 13-year-olds and younger. "Parents should set moral standards" —certainly, but prohibition without explanation rarely works, and what if peer pressure proves stronger? No wonder good and caring parents privately look on their children's sexual development with alarmed resignation: why must they start this when they haven't finished school? Just how unwise can kids get? Others treat it with denial—not my kids, or at least not yet. Or they may be confident in their moral training, in their children, and in the good relationships which, they feel, must lead those children to confide in them.

We forget our own adolescence too quickly. All adolescence, especially, perhaps, when social forces hurry it on too soon, can be a major time of stress. It is also a time of becoming separate and becoming a person. In that undertaking one does not proceed by asking parents first. Think back to those years in your own life, remembering that choices were fewer then and came much later: pressures, temptations and opportunities were less, though they were there and often frightening. Adults are uncomfortable about giving sexual information. Adolescents are uncomfortable seeking it. *However* good the relationship, an adolescent's first sexual experience, at any age, is rarely discussed with parents ahead of time. Often it was unexpected: if half-expected, talking about the prospect to parents raises a threat of losing face if nothing happens, plus the risk of an avoidable lecture if parents don't approve. Part of this concern is self-serving—part is real consideration for you— "Why worry them? It would blow their minds."

We have to face the fact, as parents, that adolescents rarely ask for advice until some sexual experience has actually occurred, and often not before it has happened several times. In preadolescence encounters with sexuality are unplanned—wet dreams, menstruation, the discovery of masturbation. Preinformation here serves to prevent damaging anxiety over natural processes. In later adolescence, sex means other people. It becomes a part of expectation, fantasy and planning even when the first physical encounter is unexpected—as it usually is. Any advice or counsel in this area *must* be in place before need arises if it is to serve any useful purpose— before the pressures of puberty mount: before the natural wish to be one's own man, one's own woman, hinders communication with parents. It has to be there beforehand, even if it is only to serve as damage control—still more if it is to help in forming responsible moral choices and decently considerate behavior. Not all children will "need it" early, or even, while still children, at all, though all will need it eventually. You cannot tell ahead of time, however, how or when need will arise.

The separateness of adolescence has always grieved and frightened parents, yet it is a necessary part of human growth. Even in a family which holds and shares strong traditional religious standards, for instance, this is so, and nowhere better expressed than in Luke *15* 11-23. The prodigal son (or daughter) epitomizes not only human frailty but the drama of growing up.

Children need both limit-setting and the benefit of their parents' experience of life. The best social education, not only in matters of sexuality, is nonverbal—seeing that parents love one another and value affectionate contact as a way of showing it. With this object lesson in living as a foundation they still need factual information and above all the opportunity to talk. If they cannot talk to you, they will talk to others, including peers who are under the same stresses as they are (and boast about imaginary exploits), and exploitive or restrictive adults who may do harm. Not all parents have themselves found sexual living easy. Children will respect frankness, however, if we say so—they are already our sharpest, but not unsympathetic, observers. Discomfort in talking about such matters can be overcome: what matters most is not saying "the right thing" but saying what you really think. Children penetrate game-playing with uncanny skill. If you say "yes" and look "no," or say "no" and act "yes," they reject the preachment for the underlying attitude. Conservative or liberal, religious or secular, the fact of conveying what you genuinely believe is the "right" sex education for your children. Whether or not they accept your standards in the long run they will respect and thank you for being honest with them.

Frankness can itself be testing to adults. We have talked to liberal parents who would not give a book such as this to their children for fear of being asked, for example, "Did *you* have sex before marriage?" It's tough to say "None of your business" or "Yes, but we don't recommend it," or "Yes, and it was fine," or "Yes, but we wouldn't be comfortable if you did," or "No, we certainly did not." It is easier, we realize, to be frank in theory than in practice.

You can use books as messengers to your children, but most parents will not wish to leave it all to authors, any more than to teachers. Books should be a bridge to discussion. Children assume that what is on the printed page can be talked about, or it would not be there. They also tend to treat books as final authorities. This should be discouraged. Books help timid children to ask questions and galvanize timid parents to answer them, apart from being a resource on facts—we are not all encyclopedias. Books are not a substitute for parenting, but they can be a help in this difficult area. We have written this book with care, hoping that you will find it useful in meeting the task.

A Note on Contraception

It has to be assumed that many adolescents are going to experiment with sex. It is therefore vital that they should be aware of what methods there are and how they work. Equally whatever decision parents take in the matter of contraception, they should be aware of the medical facts on which our advice in the book is based.

If prevention of pregnancy is the overriding consideration, the Pill is the method of choice. Oral contraceptives are, with proper prescription, problem-free in the adolescent period—widely-publicised doubts about their effects and side-effects apply almost entirely to later, adult use over long periods. Youngsters can take advantage of their high reliability. Current research has not produced any reason why, if it is prescribed with proper medical precautions, an effective low-estrogen pill should not be used safely by adolescents to cover the early period of sexual activity. Its great advantage is that if it is taken as prescribed it will work. It may not be the best contraceptive to use throughout life. A girl who initially uses it should review other methods with a physician as she becomes more mature. The risk of adverse effects is greatest in later life. Parents should *not* provide supplies of the Pill without medical consultation.

Intrauterine devices ("loops") are not commonly prescribed to cover early adolescence. All other effective methods, including the diaphragm, depend for their reliability on proper care and technique. We have emphasized the sheath-plus-foam method, because it is virtually the only effective form of birth control which teenagers can use without adult help and with a reasonable prospect of protection. Sheath alone and foam alone are better than nothing, but carry a higher risk of failure than the combination of both. Whereas the Pill gives virtually complete protection against pregnancy provided it is correctly and conscientiously swallowed on schedule, the success figures for all mechanical methods depend on the intelligence and diligence of the user, often under what may be difficult circumstances. Our aim has been to provide as much security as is possible, and incidentally sharing of responsibility between boy and girl.

16

CONTENTS

CONTENTS

SEX IS...

"Sex" is something people talk about a great deal—like the weather, or politics. Some folk are extremely scared of it—they talk about "sex and violence" or "sex and drugs" as if it were some kind of social problem.

The word "sex" simply refers to the fact that people come in two kinds, male and female. But often when people talk about sex, they mean the fact that male and female get together to produce a baby: or they are talking about the physical acts, and the feelings and desires, which bring this about. They can also mean the whole set of rules, customs, fears and beliefs about what men and women do together. Learning about sex involves learning about all these different things.

The most obvious thing about a man's and a woman's sexual organs is that they fit together. That is what having two separate sexes is about. The fitting-together of the sex parts of a man and a woman is how every human life is set going. But people also often do the same thing for reasons other than wanting to make a baby, because the feelings it gives them are so good and the whole experience is so enjoyable. Most of the sex people have is for pleasure, and not to have babies. The process of fitting together by putting the penis into the vagina is called intercourse or sexual intercourse. Every person you see—including people who are scared about sex, or think it is sinful or "not quite nice"—is here only because some man and some woman had sexual intercourse together.

Another word for intercourse is "coitus," which rhymes with "know it, Gus." It simply means the same thing in Latin.

People used to think that it was better if youngsters didn't know anything about sexual behavior or were told fairy-stories about it— that babies were brought by storks or found under bushes. Most children enjoy stories, but those adults must have forgotten their own young days, if they imagined that any but very young children believed these things. We think that "sex" is so important and enjoyable that everyone should know quite early in life what it is all about. "Sex" includes many of the best experiences one can have in life— like being lovers, being married, having children. It's also quite as exciting as a Moon landing—more so, because unlike a Moon landing we all of us, when we are grown up, get to take part in sex if we choose.

As we said, "sex" simply refers to the fact that people come in two kinds, male and female. At birth they don't differ very greatly, except in the parts they will use later on to express sexuality ("to have sex"). The baby boy has his sex equipment showing. The baby girl's sexual equipment can't be seen so easily because much of it is inside. But the opening leading to it, the vulva, can be seen as a fold or crack. The vulva is the way into a soft passage, the vagina, which leads to the womb, the place where babies develop. Vagina (which rhymes with Dinah) is Latin for "sheath."

As growth goes on, the two sexes get less alike in body. They also get less alike because in our society (and in most others) people often dress them differently and teach them different things. Often

Growing up—the changes which take place between small child and adult

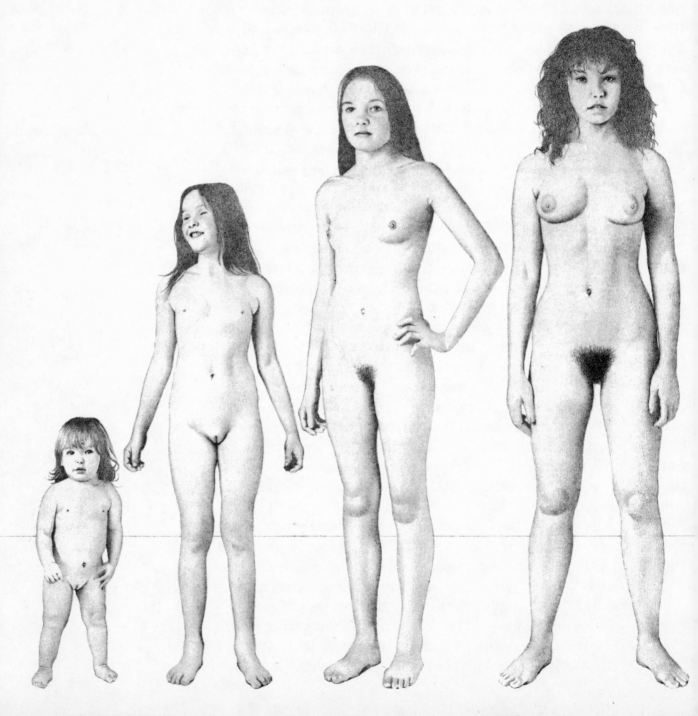

the different ways in which boys and girls, or men and women, behave aren't due to built-in differences between them but to what they have been taught is "manly" or "feminine." These learned ways of acting are called sex roles (like the role, or part, an actor plays on the stage).

Our pictures show the two sexes from baby to adult, without their clothes. The biggest changes happen any time between age 11 and age 16, when both sexes start to develop adult characteristics.

The changes happen at different ages in different people—usually they happen most rapidly between the ages of 13 and 15

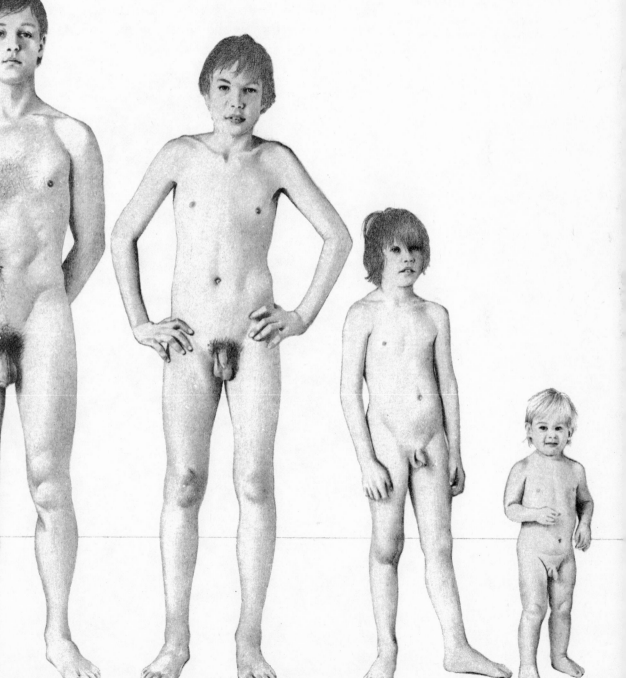

We have written this book both for young people who are not yet having sex and not yet really ready to have it, and for older teenagers as well. Most of the trouble and anxiety which some youngsters have when they do reach the "sex age" comes from not knowing *ahead of time* the facts about human sex behavior. People ought not to have sex at all with other people until they are ready for it—any more than they should try to drive until they are ready for it and can do it without hurting themselves and other people. But it is a good idea to know all about it. This not only prepares you for it when you do become ready, whenever that is, it stops you from believing nonsense you hear from people who don't know the facts, and it explains why one can only really enjoy sex if one acts responsibly.

You need to understand what you are doing before you start to do it. This is true in dealing with things—it is even more true when one is dealing with people

Talking About Sex

The sex parts and actions have names, naturally. The trouble is that until lately people weren't supposed ever to talk about them—except for doctors, who used Latin names. People did, of course, talk about them nonetheless, but the common names they used got labeled "rude" or "dirty," and people still freak out if you use them. We've used the long Latin names here, because you might as well know them, but you'll probably use the other words too. Here are some:

intercourse, coitus . . . . . fucking, balling, getting laid

masturbation . . . . jerking off, beating one's meat

penis . . . . cock, prick

testicles . . . . balls

scrotum . . . . bag

vulva . . . . cunt, pussy, box

have an orgasm, climax . . . . come

sperm, semen . . . . come, jism

erection . . . . hard-on, boner

If you look at these words, you will see there is nothing "rude" about them, any more than there is about any other word. Either they are names of other things used for something sexual (a "prick" is an old word for a cattle prod) or they are very ancient words for sexual organs. For example, "cunt" means "that which is typical of a woman." It is really the same word as "queen," and simply means "womanhood." "Pussy" is an old word for a hare or rabbit—something to do here with soft hair and having a burrow. Quite a lot of other body parts have slang or joke names—breasts get called "tits," "knockers" and "boobs."

Everybody gets to hear these words. You can use any words you choose, but you need to be careful to whom you are talking. The Latin words are safe with anyone who is able to talk about sex at all without getting upset.

Obviously, since sex is an important matter, one needs to be able to talk about it, and to have a suitable set of words for the purpose which don't interfere with sensitive discussion because the words themselves freak people out.

WHAT PUBERTY IS

Boy and girl babies are pretty much alike: boy and girl children are often dressed differently and may do different things. But the big change comes when boys start to turn into men, and girls into women. Of course this happens gradually. You don't go to bed one night as a child and wake up next morning as a grown-up person. But when it starts to happen, the boy or girl notices it, and so may other people. For instance, a little girl, who has had a flat chest like a boy until then, will notice that her breasts have started to grow. The first

thing a boy notices is that his penis is getting bigger. The whole change-over to being a man or a woman takes several years. Once it has started it goes ahead quite steadily. It's important to know that some people start quite early and others quite late, in terms of birthdays. You may find you start later or earlier than other boys and girls whom you know. This does not matter at all—you will all get to the same place in the end. Often boys, just before they start to get man-shaped, go through a period when they get a little girl-shaped, with more fat than muscle. Grown-ups call this "puppy fat," and before long the boy begins to grow and it goes away.

Girls usually develop faster than boys, though there are big differences among different people. Just before this big change, called puberty or adolescence, both sexes put on fat and get rounder in the limbs. Girls keep this rounder outline on into womanhood; boys tend to lose it when they grow muscle. How fast people develop depends partly on how well fed they are, but in a country where most people are reasonably well fed, the chief factor is the setting of their internal "clock." There are some families and some people in whom puberty comes very early, others for whom it is late, so if you look around any class of 15-year-olds you will see some who look like boys and some who are obviously young men, already shaving, some who are girls and some who are almost women. Being early or late makes no difference to the end result, however—the late starters make just as good men and women by the time they catch up.

These children are in fact all the same age—you can see how some are developing faster than others

The Clock Starts

The "clock" which starts puberty rolling is situated in the brain (in a part called the hypothalamus). It acts rather like the alarm in the radio which turns on the music when it is time to wake up. This "clock" turns on the production of hormones. Hormones are chemical substances released into the blood which pass on orders to other parts of the body. In this case they switch on the ovaries in the girl, and the testicles in the boy. The ovaries are the small organs inside the abdomen which contain the egg cells, which are the female contribution to any future baby. The testicles are the two rubbery knobs in the scrotum which hurt if you squeeze them. These produce the sperms—very tiny swimming cells with long tails, which are the male's contribution to any future baby. One ovum plus one sperm makes one baby. Once puberty has taken place, the hormone cycles begin, and before long, though not always in the first few cycles, the girl will shed one ovum a month. The girl's supply of ova is already complete at birth—and will last her for life: she does not make any more of them. The boy starts to produce sperms at puberty in enormous numbers, and will go on producing them all his life. The main result, when the "alarm" rings to show that it is time for puberty, is that the ovary and the testicles each start on their other main job, that of producing the female and male sex hormones; it is these hormones that bring about the visible changes which make it clear to everyone that the person is becoming adult.

Changes in a part of the brain, the hypothalamus, trigger a chain of chemical signals which turn on the girl's ovaries and the boy's testicles

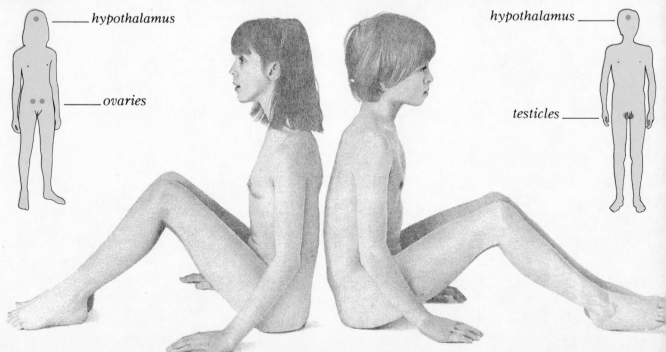

hypothalamus

ovaries

hypothalamus

testicles

The First Changes

The first change you see when puberty starts is that girls start to get breasts, and boys start to get bigger testicles and a bigger penis. Then the sex hormones make boys grow muscle, while girls develop curves. Later on, boys start to get hair on their faces. Their voice-boxes grow too, so that their voices break and after a rather odd-sounding period get deeper. In both sexes hair starts to grow under the arms and around the sex organs. There isn't much of this at first, but when puberty is over it will look like our picture. Hair round the sex organs ("pubic hair") has different patterns in men and women. Some men, if they are hairy people, get hair on their limbs and chests. (Girls actually have skin hairs too, if you look closely, but they don't usually show so much unless the hairs are very dark.) Before long, too, the skin starts producing its adult layer of lubricant. This can be an awkward time, because when it starts, both sexes are apt to get pimples on the face and elsewhere ("acne"). Luckily these go away before puberty is finished in most people. All this time the breasts in the girl have been getting larger and her hips rounder. The woman's pelvis is in fact wider than a man's, to leave room for a baby to pass through—nearly everyone you see has passed through a woman's pelvis in being born. The exceptions are, of course, people who are born by what is called Caesarian section—that is, by a surgical operation, when for any reason the baby cannot be born in the usual way. As a result of having this wider pelvis, her thighs slope more (if they didn't she would have a gap between her knees) and her arms spread more from the elbows (so that they don't bump into her hips when she walks).

The pictures on the following pages show how the shapes of the two sexes change over the period of puberty, but the order in which the changes happen, the age at which they happen, and how soon they are finished may be quite different in different people.

It feels a little strange to find that you have started to develop breasts, or that you are growing hair on your body, or, if you are a boy, that your voice starts to change. So it is not surprising if young people take a little while to get used to the new, grown-up persons they are becoming.

When puberty is well along, each sex, boy and girl, has a landmark which shows that development is really progressing. These landmarks are called ejaculation (for the boy) and menstruation, or "starting periods" (for the girl). We'll explain these next, after the pictures which show what happens at puberty point by point.

34

Face becomes fuller

Possible acne

Voice deepens slightly

Upper arms become fatter

Underarm hair appears
Nipples stand out

Enlargement of breasts

Growth of pubic hair
Genitals become fleshier
and darken

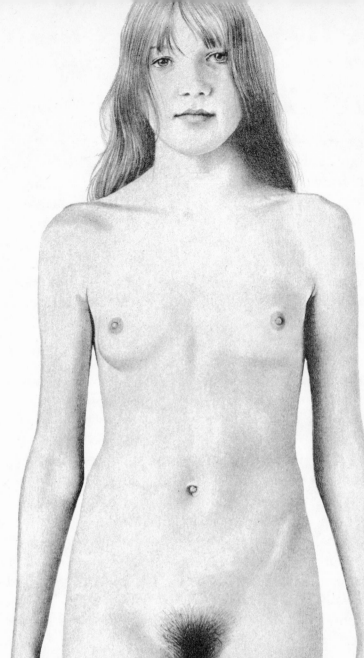

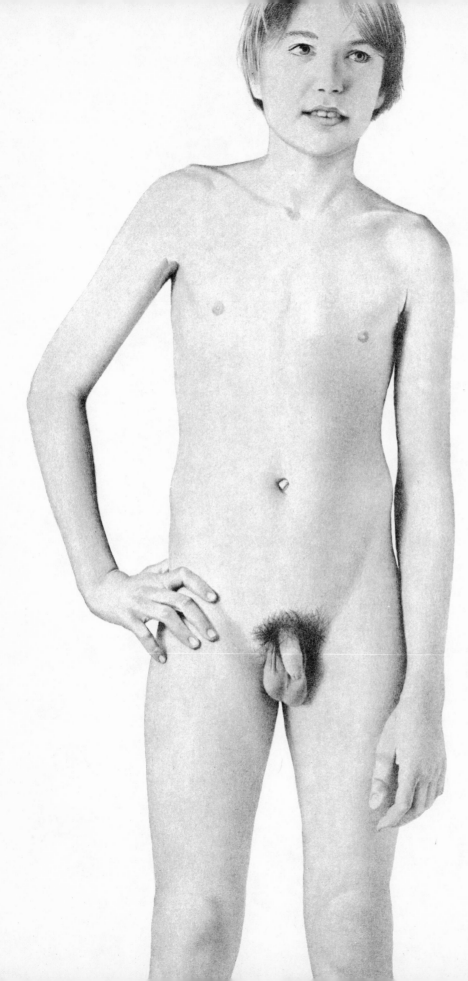

Facial hair appears

Possible acne

Voice breaks/deepens

Shoulders broaden

Underarm hair appears

Arms become thicker and more muscular

Growth of pubic hair

Penis grows bigger and darkens
Enlargement of testicles

Legs become more muscular

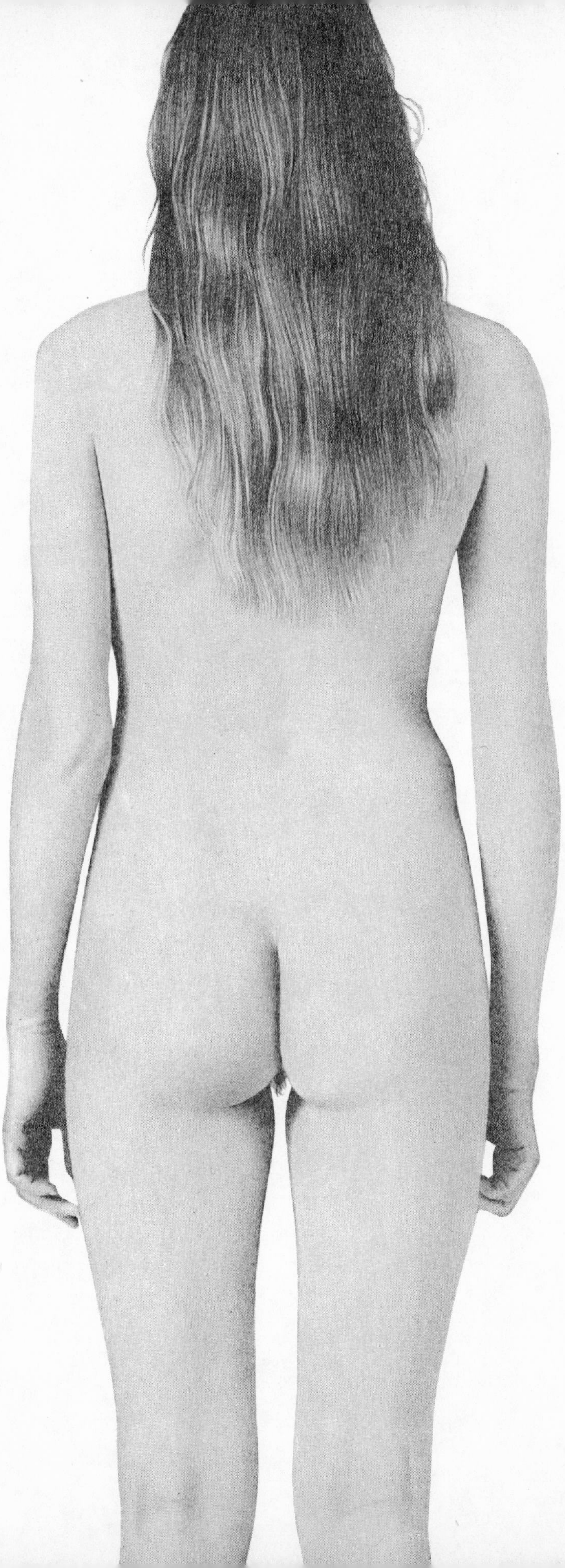

Skin becomes oilier
and coarser

Increase in height and
weight, female "figure"

Increased sweating generally

Hair on arms increases

Buttocks become fatter

Hips and thighs become fatter

Hair on legs grows

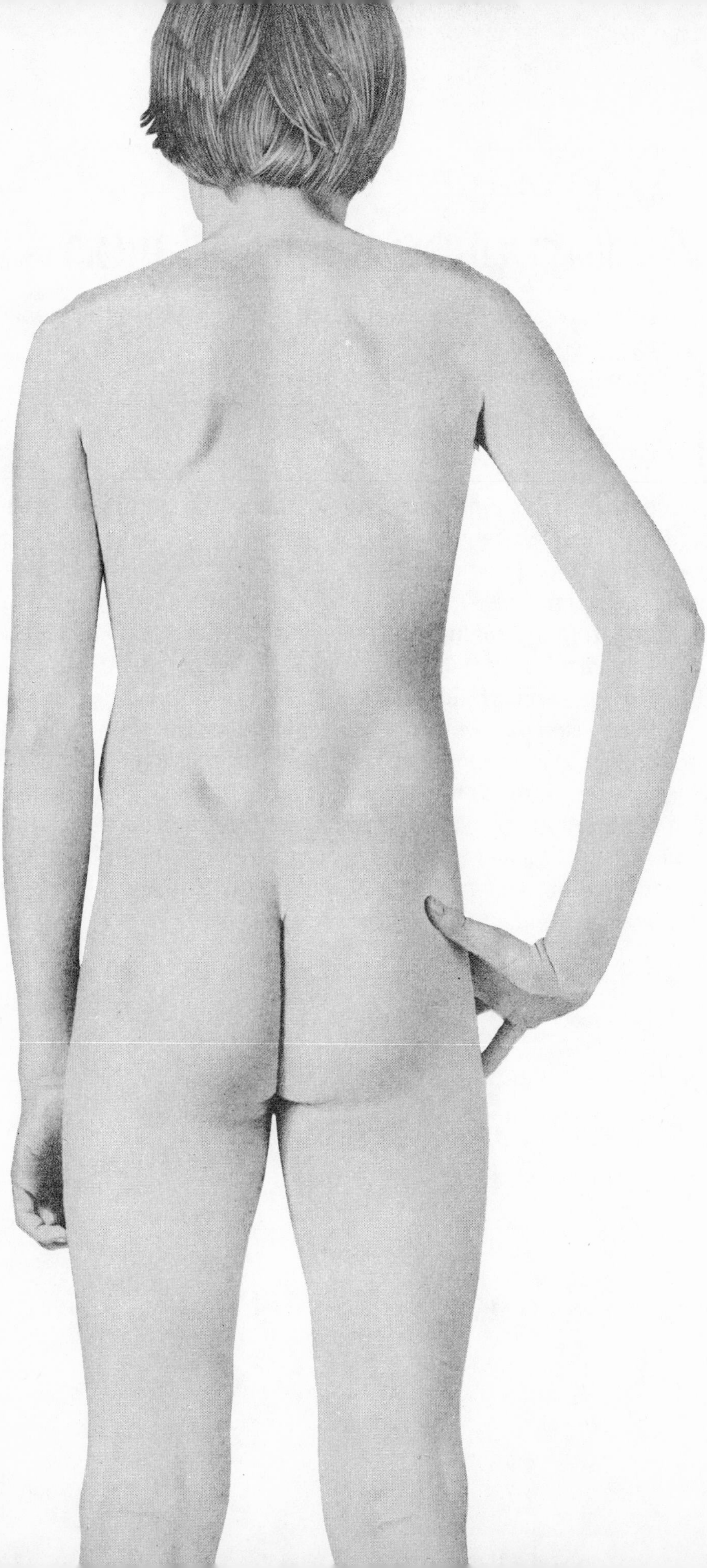

Skin becomes oilier
and coarser

Increase in height and weight,
development of male muscle
pattern

Hair growth on chest and
back

Increased sweating generally

Hair on arms increases

Hair on legs grows

38

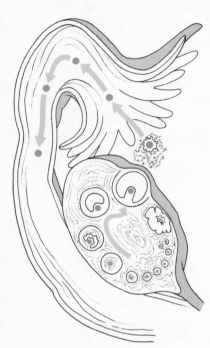

(Above) At ovulation the ovum travels out of the ovary into the tube leading to the womb (called the Fallopian tube, after the Italian anatomist who discovered it)

LANDMARKS:
Menstruation & Ejaculation

There are two events, one in each sex, which show that puberty has really occurred. The girl will menstruate for the first time, and the boy will ejaculate for the first time.

1 Menstruation

In every adult woman from puberty to about the age of 50 there is a continual development and shedding of the layer of cells which lines the womb—except when she is pregnant, and the womb has a baby in it. Every time these cells are shed—about every 28 days—there is bleeding from the vagina. This is called "having a period." The first time this happens, girls who don't expect it are apt to be scared and think there is something wrong.

The reason that women menstruate is this. Before each ovum is produced, the inside lining of the womb thickens to provide a place where, if the ovum were fertilized, it could develop. In humans and in monkeys and apes, if the ovum is not fertilized, this extra lining peels off and comes away at regular intervals. It is this regular spring-cleaning which produces the menstrual period. Cats, dogs and most other animals don't menstruate.

The girl's menstrual cycle:

At menstruation (lasting about four days in many women) the whole lining of the womb is shed. On about the fifth day a new lining starts to grow. An ovum begins to ripen in the ovary. About 14-15 days before the next period is due, the ovum leaves the ovary. The womb has a new thick lining ready to receive the ovum if it has been fertilized. At the end of the cycle the ovum, if it has not been fertilized, disappears and another period takes place

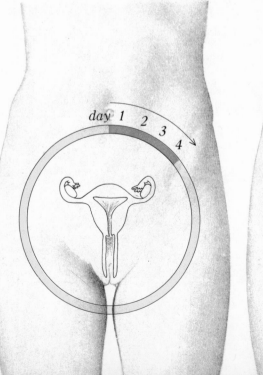

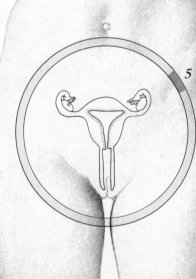

It pays to know that periods are not always regular when they first begin. Other girls you know may start earlier, or later, than you do, have longer or shorter periods, and more or fewer days in between.

Bleeding every month for a few days is a nuisance. Women often refer to their monthly period as "the curse" for this reason, and also because while it is going on they often get pains, called "cramps." These happen because the uterus is pushing out pieces of its worn-out lining. Often the best way of stopping these period pains is exercise. Just before a period the amount of water in the body increases; some people feel odd or headachy at this time.

For some reason humans have often been very puzzled about what is going on when a woman has a period. They have thought of the whole business as bad magic. It used to be believed that if a girl made bread when she had a period, the bread wouldn't rise: if she made jam, the jam wouldn't keep—and so on. Some tribal peoples made her stay by herself until it was over.

You still hear quite a lot of things about periods which are really based on magic. The ideas that you shouldn't swim, or wash your hair or take a bath when you have a period are some of these. In fact, having a period need make absolutely no difference to anything a girl does—except that she needs to put a tampon in her vagina, or a pad over her vulva, to absorb the bleeding. Having periods is an absolutely normal part of being a woman. It may be tiresome or embarrassing if you bleed suddenly, but it's not an illness and it's not bad magic. All grown women have to deal with periods.

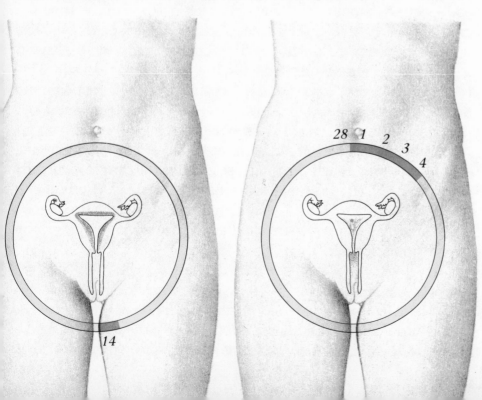

Every woman's experience of having periods is very much her own. They usually occur every 28 days, but in some people it is 26, in others 30—you get to know your own personal pattern. The bleeding usually lasts about four days, but for some people it is only one, for others as many as seven, or it may vary from time to time. Periods usually start when a girl is from 12 to 14, but they can start earlier or later. How much people bleed also varies from person to person. For most girls the amount isn't more than can be soaked up by putting tampons in the vagina. A tampon is a special wad of absorbent cotton, which can be put in easily, and has a string on it like a tail so that you can pull it out and flush it away. Young girls who have never had intercourse can usually use tampons—the instructions are on the pack. There may be a little difficulty the first time, but this soon goes: one can get small ones. People who bleed a lot may need to put a sanitary pad over the vulva as well. Mothers usually help in learning to manage all this.

A woman stops having periods around the age of 45 to 50. This stopping is called menopause, or "change of life." It doesn't mean that she stops enjoying sex—only that when the periods have stopped, she cannot have a baby, because she no longer sheds any ova.

2 Ejaculation

Boys aren't often scared by their first ejaculation, because it feels so good—better than anything they ever felt before. All the time the penis has been getting bigger, it has also been getting more sensitive, and it feels good when touched. If it is touched, and often if it isn't, it also from time to time quite suddenly gets much larger and stiff. This is called an erection. Even very small babies often get erections, and all males get them in sleep. At puberty, they occur more and more often at other times, even in class, when they can be embarrassing. Eventually, either during a dream, or because when handling the penis the boy finds that the feeling is so good that he can't stop rubbing it, he suddenly gets a super-good sensation, unlike any other, and some fluid spurts out. This is called ejaculation, and the super-good sensation is called an orgasm or climax. Those mean that the boy is now becoming a man.

The first time a boy ejaculates, what comes out is usually a slightly sticky, clear fluid, but later it gets milky and thick in appearance. This slightly salty, pleasant-smelling fluid is called sperm or semen—its old name was simply "seed." There is usually a teaspoonful or less at each ejaculation, though there may be more. It comes out in a series of spurts, and it is full of sperms, in the plural, or spermatozoa. These are small swimming half-cells which look under the microscope like rather rangy tadpoles. Another name for these is spermatozoa. It's a little confusing that the fluid is often called sperm, and the cells it contains are called sperms, but it was only about 300 years ago that the small swimming cells were first seen, by the man who invented the microscope. Sperms are the things which can fertilize an ovum and set it developing into a person, and there are hundreds of millions in every ejaculate. Semen has nothing to do with urine, even though the two come out of the same passage along the penis.

If a boy or a man who is producing sperms doesn't masturbate or have intercourse, the sperms will eventually be ejaculated during sleep, often during a dream about sex. This is called a "wet dream"— you wake up and find that you have ejaculated. This is a normal experience for all males, though if people masturbate or have sex very often it will not happen, or happen less frequently.

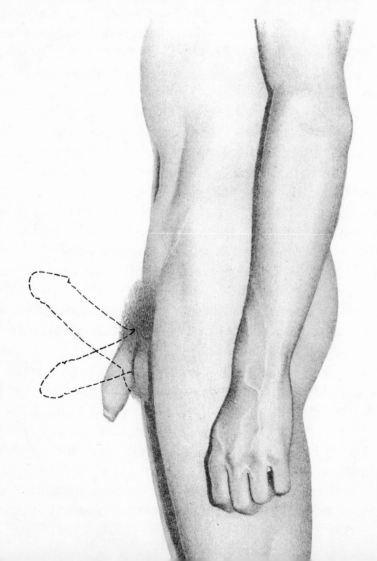

During an erection the boy's penis becomes hard and a great deal larger. Ejaculation doesn't occur whenever there is an erection, but the penis usually has to be erect before ejaculation happens. The diagram looks a little funny, but we had to show you what an erection is like.

MASTURBATION

Getting an orgasm by rubbing the sex organs is called "masturbation." It's the natural way of testing the equipment, apart from being very enjoyable, and the way that nearly all boys and many girls first learn what "sex" feels like. Even babies enjoy rubbing their sex organs if nobody stops them. Very unfortunately, and for reasons it is hard to understand, people have made an enormous fuss about this rather obvious way of practicing for adult sexuality. Some religions have called it sinful. Old books contained hair-raising nonsense about it causing blindness, insanity, and so on. If this were true, most people would be blind, insane, and so on, including the people who wrote the books. Masturbation is in fact a healthy and extremely enjoyable act. During puberty, you can use it as a kind of practice for adult sex, but it's something you will enjoy all your life, even when you are able to have adult sex as well.

Nearly all boys learn to masturbate as soon as they reach puberty. It's untrue that you can do it too often, and that this is harmful. The worst that will happen is that you might get a little sore. Boys usually masturbate by rubbing the penis up and down until they ejaculate. It's a good idea to learn to make the build-up part of the good sensation last, as this will make you enjoy adult sex more. You can keep a handkerchief ready to catch the ejaculate when you finally "come," so as not to make a mess. The liquid can spurt several feet, and there can be quite a lot of it. Although it's perfectly clean it can make spots.

A piece of nonsense one finds in old books, and which some boys and men still believe, is that "loss of semen" is weakening or harmful, and that to ejaculate often—whether in sleep, by masturbating, or by having intercourse—will make them weak. Probably they imagine that since semen is such powerful stuff—it can make babies—it is a kind of life-juice. You can no more lose too much semen than you can lose too much spit. Most of the fluid, apart from the sperms, is very like spit in composition. If you ejaculate often, the number of sperms in each ejaculation will get fewer and you will end up ejaculating mostly water and salts. People who claim they are tired after ejaculating a lot may be tired because they believe that losing semen is bad magic. This is rubbish. Having a good ejaculation may make you pleasantly sleepy for a bit, but being tired has nothing to do with how often you ejaculate.

Girls may not learn to masturbate until later, and some not until they are much older. Although there is no must about this, in both sexes learning to masturbate at puberty and really enjoying it probably helps to make later sexual relations, with another person, more pleasant.

Girls who masturbate either stroke the lips of the vulva, and the little sensitive organ called the clitoris, with the fingers, or rub their thighs together. They need to explore what makes them feel good, and this is often a little more complicated than it is in boys, but all girls can experience orgasm (or "climax") in this way if they want to. The girl's sex organs, and her breasts, feel good when touched. She can get an orgasm which feels as good as the boy's by gently rubbing them, but she doesn't ejaculate. Probably more boys than girls find out for themselves about orgasm early in puberty; some do so well before puberty, though they can't then ejaculate. It is this super-good sensation which plays such a big part in later sex life for both sexes. It's hard to describe a sensation. For the boy it is like a sneeze, in that it builds up and explodes, but if sneezing felt so good all boys would have permanent colds. For the girl it's even harder to describe, but it feels just as good. In any case, it is a fine way of learning to enjoy your body.

Obviously, masturbating is something one does in private—not because it's a nasty secret, which it isn't, but because you don't want to be disturbed, and the idea freaks some people out. It's good practice to learn early that sexual behavior calls for tact and privacy if you want to avoid upsetting other folk.

WHAT'S DIFFERENT

By the end of puberty you have not a boy and a girl but a man and a woman. It's interesting to see how they differ, apart from obvious things like breasts or no breasts, and things which they do from custom. For example, it used to be usual for men to cut their hair short, and women to grow it long. It does naturally grow longer in women, possibly to give a baby something to hold on to, but now one can't always tell males and females apart from behind. These customs change from time to time—George Washington and Davy Crockett both had long hair. Apart from the man being usually taller and having bigger muscles, the main built-in difference is that the woman is wider in the hips. This is the reason that women used sometimes to be called "broads"—you might as well call men "narrows." Women's skin is softer, the body hair pattern is different, and women don't grow beards. They also don't get bald as they grow older, whereas many men do. The different texture of woman compared with man is due to the fact that her skin has more fat under it.

WHAT'S THE SAME

Where men and women *don't* differ because of the way they are made is in being smarter, braver, timider, more likely to cry and get upset, or being better drivers or plane pilots than each other. If they come ever to differ in these ways it's because somebody taught them they ought to, and they believe it. How men and women act in a given society depends on what they have learned, not on bodily differences. In other words, sex roles are learned in childhood, not built in like a large or small pelvis.

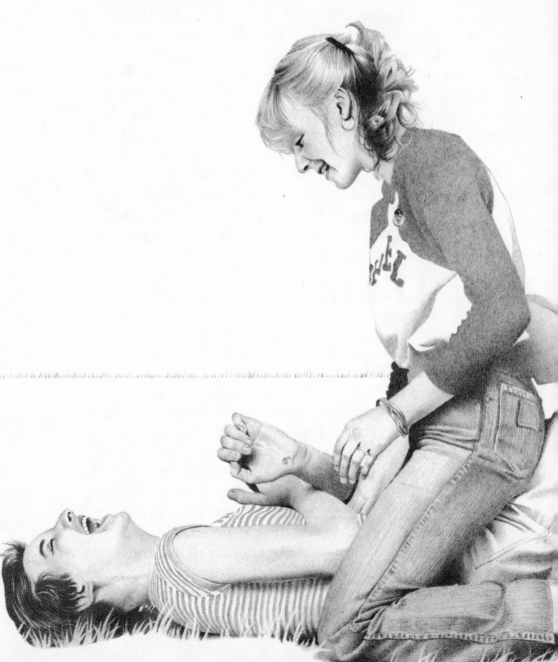

NO HURRY!

Once the girl starts menstruating and the boy can ejaculate, they know they are growing up, and they think it's great to feel they are adults, but in fact they have quite a way to go yet: there is a great deal of growing and learning still ahead of them. In order to be sexually adult they need to get together, which involves learning a lot about people and how to treat them, and though they are physically able to produce a baby between them, it would be idiotic for them to do so, and grossly unfair to the baby (who is a person too, and needs adult parents, not learners).

When you learn to fly, you don't get straight into any airplane and take off solo. When you learn to use your sexual powers, you don't start by trying to have sexual intercourse with somebody. Most youngsters start by learning how to treat their own bodies, which is why masturbation is an important part of learning. After that, they usually learn about other people—little by little. They start making friends of the opposite sex, singly or as one of a group, dating them, getting to know about them, and how to treat them. In the past, as

they got older still, this went on to kissing and holding hands—now it often also goes on to "petting," which means cuddling and touching each other, and finally touching one another's sex organs—finding out what makes another person feel good. All these things are very pleasant—it would be silly to be in such a hurry to "have sex," meaning intercourse, that one missed them. In fact they are a way of "having sex." There is absolutely no need to be in a rush to go on and have intercourse, and a great many people, boys and girls, very wisely don't go on to have intercourse until they are a lot older and really able to handle it. Petting can make a person very excited, and if it has to be stopped short, without a climax, that can be unpleasant, but two young people can perfectly well learn to give each other a climax with their hands. Or, of course, they can masturbate separately afterwards. It is probably better to do this than simply to get excited and then be "left hanging." In the past some youngsters have become so good at turning off their sex response for fear of "going too far" that when the time came to have intercourse they have had trouble staying turned on and enjoying it fully.

Of course boys and girls, when they're learning about each other, are curious and want to experiment, but the important part of curiosity is learning how to talk and listen to somebody. You need to find out what the other person likes and let him or her know what you like— not only sexually but in other ways. You learn to go along with what they want without letting them boss you, showing them what you yourself want, and generally finding out about them as people. If you treat exploring sex as a part of this, fine. If you think only about sex, as if that was the only part of boy–girl relations, you can end by treating the other person like a vending machine—you put in a dime and out comes a climax, or your partner does the same to you.

Hardly any two people like to make love in exactly the same way. So nobody can write a book of instructions saying "Girls like..." or "Boys like..." which would make you a "good lover" if you read it. A good lover is someone who can talk to other people and listen to

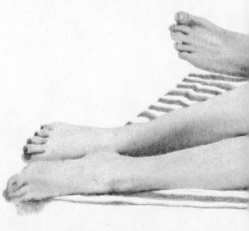

what they say, and find out what they enjoy most.

Most girls find that boys are in too much of a hurry to put the penis in the vagina and "have sex" like that. Often they prefer a good deal of gentle touching and kissing first. Every time two people make love, each has to find out what pleases the other most. Of course when two people have been lovers for a long time they get to know this, but even then they can still find ways of pleasing one another that they didn't know about before. It's a mistake for the man to be in a great hurry to "have intercourse." It's a mistake for the woman to think she ought to lie back and leave it all to the man. Making love is something two people do *for one another*, not something that one person does to another person. Two people who can't tell one another what they like, after they've got over the first shyness, probably shouldn't be making love at all.

THE HARDWARE

We now need to look in detail at the "hardware" with which men and women are equipped for sex. We have given the names of some of the items already. You can see the others in these diagrams.

1 Women

Apart from her breasts, and the lips of the vulva, you can't usually see much of the girl's equipment, any more than you can see her tonsils. If you open the lips of the vulva you can, however, see the inner lips, the clitoris (which is a little, smooth, very sensitive knob) and the way into the vagina. In young girls this is often partly closed by a little skin fold, called the hymen. When the woman has had a lot of sexual intercourse, the hymen may get torn or stretched, though one can sometimes still find it after she has had a baby. In the old days it was thought that on the first occasion she had intercourse, it ought to be torn, and she ought to bleed, proving that it *was* the first time. This rarely happens now—all it shows is that when a girl has intercourse the first time the man needs to go gently so as not to make her sore. Not even a doctor can tell for sure by looking at the hymen who has had intercourse and who hasn't.

A woman needs to know what her sex organs look like and where they are. The best way to find out is to use a hand mirror. See if you can find all the parts shown in the diagram. (All people look different down there.)

A woman's sex organs can really only be seen if they are held open, as in this illustration. A woman can see her own structure if she uses a mirror

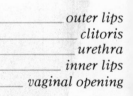

outer lips
clitoris
urethra
inner lips
vaginal opening

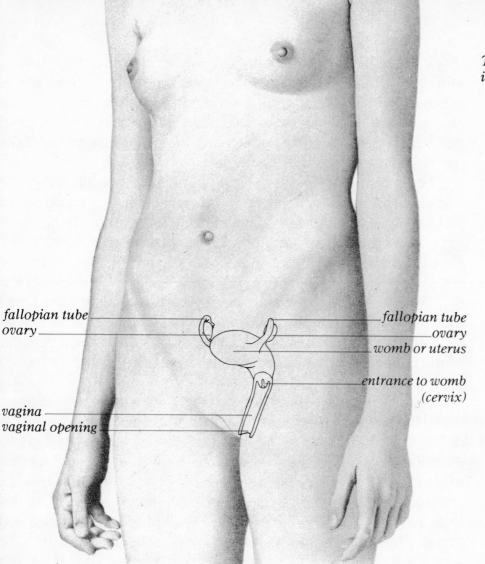

fallopian tube
ovary

fallopian tube
ovary
womb or uterus

entrance to womb
(cervix)

vagina
vaginal opening

The clitoris in girls is not easy to see because it is inside the vulva, at the front, where the two lips join. It has a smooth knob at the end (about the size of a cherry-pit in a grown woman). It is the most sensitive place in most girls, and every girl should be able to find it with her finger. It is so sensitive that it needs rather gentle touching. In making love, many girls and women enjoy having it touched, and they may touch or stroke it when they masturbate—but boys need to be sensitive and let the girl show them what gives her the best feelings. Starting off by touching the clitoris doesn't always do this: it may simply hurt. Most boys by contrast like their penis rubbed quite hard, and they may be far too rough in the way they touch the girl. Many girls prefer to be touched, not on the clitoris, but on other parts of the vulva, such as the inner lips.

It's interesting that only girls have an organ which has *no* other function beside giving them sexual pleasure—the clitoris is there simply to give good sexual feelings.

Beside the parts which one can see in a mirror, women have lubricating glands, which you can't see, but which are important. When a woman is sexually aroused and ready for intercourse, these glands moisten the way into the vagina so that the penis slips in easily, and a lot of moisture also comes through the vaginal walls. A boy becomes stiff, a girl becomes wet.

Some women get wet very easily—others, especially if they are beginners and a bit nervous, like a lot of tenderness first and then a lot of gentle touching and stroking around the vulva with the man's finger or tongue before they are ready to have his penis inside them. People who really enjoy each other's bodies enjoy this sort of play anyway.

When the lubricant glands start to work, blood is also switched into the walls of the vulva and the vagina—the skin of the vulva reddens and pads in the vaginal wall swell to make it fit comfortably round the penis. Some women also get a pink flush on the chest and back.

At some time every girl and woman has to have what is called a "pelvic examination"—as part of a medical checkup, or because the doctor needs to use it to find the cause of something. In a pelvic examination, the doctor either puts a finger into the vagina to feel the organs in your pelvis, or he may put in a spoon-shaped thing called a speculum which makes it possible for him to see inside. This is a little strange to get used to, but there is nothing to be embarrassed about. The doctor has to be able to check the sex organs just in the same way as he needs to look down your throat. Having regular pelvic examinations is important for a woman in order to keep well, and it is a good idea to get used to them fairly early, because if you are relaxed and not afraid that it will hurt it is easier for the doctor to check that all is well.

2 Men

The sexual equipment in men is easy to see, because most of it is outside: penis, scrotum, the testicles (which you can feel in the scrotum).

The testicles in men are very sensitive, and hurt badly if squeezed or struck, which is why boys wear athletic protectors. It may seem a bad idea to have such tender structures hanging around in a bag, where they can be struck. The reason is that sperm can't develop at body temperature, and the scrotum acts as a refrigerator. In many animals with a breeding season, the testicles are carried inside the body, and only come down when it is time to produce sperms. Humans have sex all the time, so the testicles are down all the time, having come down into the scrotum just before or just after birth. The "thermostat" in the scrotum keeps them at the right temperature. In hot weather the scrotum hangs lower, in cold it pulls up close to the body—during an orgasm or climax the testicles may move right up close to the pelvis into two "pods" which keep them out of the way. We often spoil the natural heat control by wearing tight clothing—sometimes this causes the testicles to stop producing sperms altogether, though if you started to think that because you wear tight pants you run no risk of getting a girl pregnant, you are very wrong indeed.

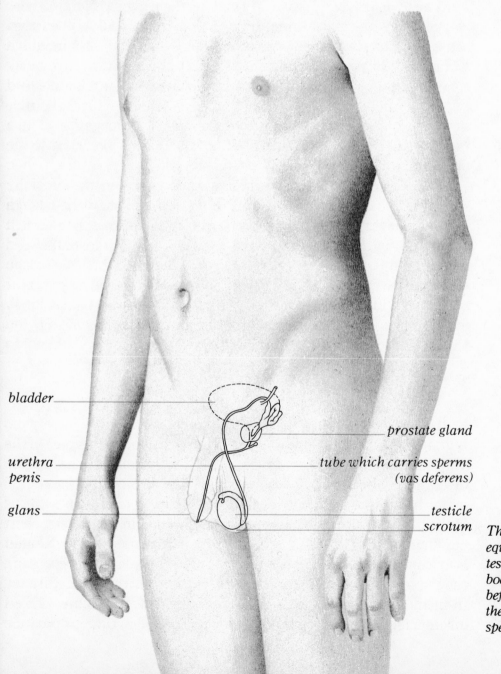

bladder

prostate gland

urethra
penis

tube which carries sperms
(vas deferens)

glans

testicle
scrotum

The man's internal equipment. Because the testicles were once inside the body and came down just before birth into the scrotum, the pipe which carries the sperm goes "up and around."

A grown man's erect penis is usually about six or seven inches long. Some are bigger and some smaller, but all kinds work equally well whatever their size. A big one only looks impressive. Some girls are scared the first time they see an erection, because it looks too big to go in without hurting; it isn't. Many boys worry that their penis is too small because they have seen other boys, in showers and locker rooms, with bigger ones. How big a penis looks when it isn't erect depends on many things. On a cold day, it may shrink right up, "so that you can't tell whether you are Arthur or Annie." A big unerect penis only enlarges less when it becomes erect.

Because some people worry about the size of their penises, all kinds of quacks advertise ways of making them bigger. None of these works, and some of the things they sell can injure you. Anyhow they are quite unnecessary—a "small" penis works fine, and men and women are designed so that they fit one another anyway. In olden times, men used to pad out their trousers to make the contents look bigger. Girls tend to worry about the size of their breasts, and they may sometimes pad their bras to make *those* look bigger. It's funny how people don't realize that all shapes and sizes look good to the opposite sex if you see them on someone you like.

The end of the penis is covered by a sheath of skin (the foreskin). At birth, this often cannot be pulled right back to show the smooth knob (glans) at the end of the penis. As the boy grows, however, it separates, and boys need to pull it back as far as it will go, so they can wash under it, when they take a bath or a shower. If they don't, dead skin and a secretion called smegma collect under it and may make it sore. In having sex, people often pull the foreskin right back, or they may prefer to use it as an introducer to make the penis slide into the vagina easily.

Circumcision

Cutting off the foreskin is called "circumcision." This is a very old human custom, though how it began nobody knows. It is part of the Jewish and of the Moslem religion for all male babies to be circumcised. Many American boys and men have also been circumcised even though they are not Jewish or Moslem. A circumcised penis looks different. Instead of ending in a tube of skin, like a very short elephant trunk, it ends in a smooth acorn-shaped knob. Neither being circumcised nor being uncircumcised makes any difference in having sex. If you are uncircumcised and you pull the skin right back from the glans, your penis will look as if it were circumcised. A circumcised penis is easier to wash, but if you have boy babies you may not want pieces to be cut off them, unless having them circumcised is a part of your religion. Most doctors now say that it is better to leave well enough alone.

Plumbing

In girls the pipe which carries the urine from the bladder is quite short and comes out in the vulva, at a little dimple between the clitoris and the entrance of the vagina. In boys it runs to the end of the penis, and is also used to carry the sperm. It may seem odd to use one pipe for both, but this is a good piece of engineering, because the longer the pipe the less easily germs get up it into the bladder. Boys do in fact get fewer bladder infections than girls. Urine and sperms cannot get mixed, because when the penis erects, there is a built-in valve which closes, to switch the plumbing from "urine jettison" to "sperm eject." This is why it is hard to urinate when you have an erection.

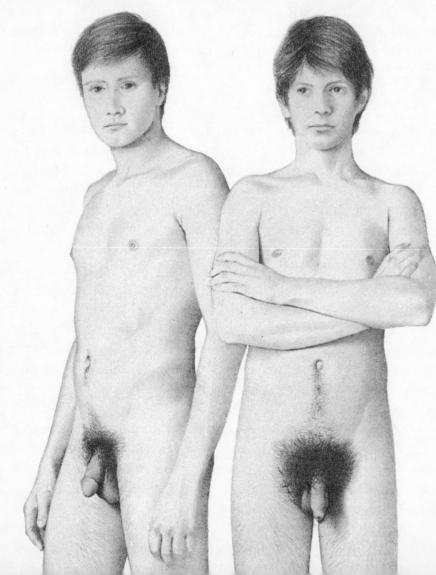

Circumcized and uncircumcized boys look different, but circumcision makes no difference to function

Erection

Erection in males can be turned on in two ways—from the brain, and from the touch organs in the penis itself. A boy can get an erection by thinking about sex or by touching, or having anything else touch, the bulb ("glans" which means "acorn") at the end of the penis, or the skin nearby. It can also happen for no obvious reason, like in class or when you are swimming, and boys very often wake in the morning with an erection. When erection occurs, blood is switched into the two hydraulics in the shaft of the penis, which act like the hydraulics in a plane landing-gear, and raise the penis into the erect position (about 45°), make it become stiff and hard, and lock it in place. There is a picture of an erect penis on page 41. After ejaculation is over, the hydraulics start to drain and the penis goes back to the resting state. Erection occurs in the same way in girls, but is harder to see, because the hydraulics are pads surrounding the vagina that get it ready for insertion. The clitoris also has small hydraulics, which erect it, and the nipples and breasts may also erect.

HAVING SEX

What actually happens when two people have intercourse? Nearly all young people are very curious about this, because it is the one important experience in life which has been kept secret and made to sound mysterious.

If a man and a woman like one another, especially if they are lovers who have often done this before, sexual feelings are easily turned on simply by being together, seeing and touching each other. In fact, people who are easily excited sexually may find this happens at times, and with people, when they are not going to make love. The boy may get an erection, the girl's vagina may become wet. In actual lovemaking, by the time they have got to undressing each other, kissing each other, handling and kissing the woman's breasts and one another's sex organs, both of them will usually be excited and ready. How quickly people become aroused can vary very much from person to person.

Pushing the penis in before the woman is ready usually hurts, and pain will stop the glands from secreting after that. So it is important for lovers to wait, not just until the man has an erection, but until the woman is excited enough to let his penis slip in comfortably. This is one reason that men who hurry make bad lovers. Quite apart from the practical matter of lubrication, hurrying spoils the pleasure of sex. People need to take time to enjoy one another. If they do feel "in a hurry" (not just both of them so excited they don't want to wait any longer) they're probably having sex at the wrong time or in the wrong place.

Finally the man slips his penis into the woman's vagina and moves it in and out, while she moves her hips; the vagina may contract and increase their sensations, and the pressure of his body on her clitoris excites her as much as the rubbing of his penis excites him. Good lovers try to make this experience last as long as possible and ensure that both reach a climax—the woman may reach more than one. They don't always do this exactly together. Finally the man will ejaculate—he may stop there and take his penis out of the vagina, or it may get soft and slip out. Often they will, if they wish it, go on caressing each other rather as they did before insertion, until the woman has had as many climaxes as she wants.

Men often reach one climax only, though many can reach a second one after a while. Women may reach one or many; some women can have so many that they don't know where one stops and the next starts. All women are different in the kind and number of climaxes they have. After his climax, the man may or may not lose his erection—some men find that the penis gets very sensitive and they need to stop for a while.

People sometimes take five minutes or less to reach climax after the penis is in the vagina. But a skilful couple can make it last very much longer than that, and give the woman time to have one or more climaxes before the man reaches his. Sometimes both of them "get there" together, but this doesn't always happen, and they need not worry if it doesn't, provided both of them feel satisfied and relaxed when they finish. This resting together often is one of the best parts of having sex—which is why it is a bad idea to hurry over it: to enjoy this they really need a place where they can relax.

People use all kinds of positions to have sex—the position with the man lying on top of the woman, between her legs, is an old favorite. It is sometimes jokingly called the "missionary position," because South Sea Islanders (who liked to have sex sitting facing each other with the woman astride) were once told by a European missionary that the man-on-top position was the "right" one. Obviously if the man is very heavy it isn't the right one—the woman may enjoy sex far more if she comes on top. People also like to have sex from behind, which is what most animals do. Experienced lovers like to take turns. Books have been written describing hundreds of different positions for sex—the only point of these is that they encourage people to see how they can best please one another.

IMPOTENCY

If a man does not get an erection when he needs one, this is called "impotency." It can be caused by drugs like alcohol which upset the mechanism, or by illness, but by far the commonest cause is worry—fear that he won't get one, wanting very much to put on a performance, being afraid someone will walk in. Nearly all men experience it sometimes. Boys quite often find they are "turned off" if they are very nervous at first intercourse, or they may "come" so quickly that they barely have time to start ("premature ejaculation"). The cure is to try again later when they aren't so uptight. The girl can help a lot by not being anxious herself or critical, and encouraging the boy to rest or sleep a bit and try later.

A woman can still manage to have sex if none of the normal excitement changes take place, but she may not then enjoy it or have good feelings from it. When a woman never enjoys sex, she used to be said to be frigid. Now we merely say that she hasn't yet learned to enjoy. Usually this happens because she has been told things about sex which have frightened or upset her. Often she has never learned to masturbate at puberty and does not really know precisely what would make her feel good. If this happens, a counselor can teach her to enjoy her body, but often she has first to get rid of a lot of notions about sex being wrong or dangerous. Most women don't enjoy sex so much with a man they don't really like, or a man who is clumsy, or if they don't feel really comfortable and can't let themselves go. This may be because somebody might walk in, or hear what is going on, for example—or, of course, because they took no precautions and might have a baby. Boys nearly always get a climax if anyone or anything stimulates their penises enough. Girls often take longer to learn what they like. If a girl doesn't enjoy sex very much the first few times that she has it, this is nothing to worry about. Every woman is just as able to enjoy sex as a man—in fact probably more able—but she often has more to learn about herself. It helps if she knows she has seen to it that there is absolutely no chance that she might have a baby. She MUST do this, if she is going to have sex at all, *until* she wants one and there are two adult parents to care for it.

WHAT SEX IS FOR

"Sex" in humans is obviously, from the look of the equipment, concerned originally with making babies—women have a womb to carry them in, and breasts for feeding them; men have sperms and a penis to put into the woman's vagina. In some animals, sex is only about having babies. But not in humans, and this is the most important thing about sex in humans—we use it for other purposes beside baby-making. This is obvious if you think that a woman is only able to be fertilized, and a baby can only be started, if sex occurs on or around the time of the month when she has shed an ovum. But humans mate much oftener than that—from twice a week to twice a day are quite common frequencies. They also mate all through pregnancy, when another baby can't be produced. They may even want to mate when the woman has her period, a time when she is not likely to conceive. By contrast many female animals will only mate when they have an ovum ready. A mare, for example, would kick a horse which tried to mate at any other time, and the horse wouldn't try. The reason some people mate so often is that it is probably one of the most enjoyable experiences one can have, and they need to have it often. For people who care about each other, every time they have sex, they are able to express that caring more and they love each other more. Sex is also tremendous fun.

Accordingly, it's said that sex in humans has three uses—reproduction, relation and recreation (in other words, babies, love and fun). And this is the origin of a lot of the crossed wires and worry which have made one of the best things in life into one of the most anxious for humans. YOU NEED TO KNOW WHICH OF THESE THREE YOU ARE AFTER, AND WHICH YOUR PARTNER IS AFTER. For a start, any time two people have sex, unless they take precautions to see that they don't have a baby (and they can easily take these) a baby may be conceived. If that happens, and all they wanted was fun, it's a disaster, and a wicked trick to play on the baby. Babies need parents for a steady 15 years or more, and if you don't aim to give them this you have no right to start one. Or suppose one partner feels that having sex is a token of great love on his or her part, imagines that the other feels the same, and finds afterwards that the partner was in it for fun, and merely wanted to play? That can give the loving partner a very bad experience. Babies, love and fun are all good uses of sexuality, and adults need it to express some or all of these at different times. They aren't incompatible. You can have love and fun, or love and fun and babies BUT YOU HAVE TO KNOW WHICH YOU BOTH WANT. There are two really wicked and immoral sexual acts, which you should be ashamed to commit if you are a human being. One is deliberately to produce, or risk producing, a baby you don't want and can't rear. The other is to treat another person as a thing simply because you like their body and want to play with them, without making sure they want that too.

WHAT SEX IS FOR:
1 Babymaking

In view of the importance of not having an unwanted baby, you need to be absolutely clear about the basic facts of baby-making.

Some girls worry that they might get pregnant because a boy kisses them—they can't. To start a baby, live sperms have to get at least into the vulva. Normally this happens because the man ejaculates inside the woman, but it isn't safe to put the penis in or near the vulva at all, or to reckon on pulling it out before ejaculation. You may be too slow, the sperm spurts out with some force, and enough of it may get into the vulva. Also there are quite often a few live sperms around, as an advance party, a long time before the main ejaculation. In petting, boys and girls often masturbate one another. If either gets sperm on the fingers and then puts the fingers into the vagina or the vulva, there is a possibility that some might reach an ovum, so with this kind of "heavy petting" you need to be extra careful. It only very rarely produces a baby but it can happen, and nobody wants to take risks. If you fully understand how pregnancy happens, you won't need to worry.

The safest thing is to be prepared for sex, if you mean to have it at all, by using proper birth control precautions. A girl can't, of course, get pregnant by kissing or sucking a boy's penis during love-play even if he ejaculates.

EVERY TIME two people have sex together, they have to decide whether what they are doing is love-making or baby-making as well, because all love-making can turn into baby-making unless the couple takes certain definite precautions to see that it doesn't. These precautions are called "birth control" (or "contraception," which means "precautions" in Latin). We will tell you a lot about these later.

Every time a man and woman, or a boy and girl, have sex together, EVEN IF IT'S THE VERY FIRST TIME, it can produce a baby, a new person, who is going to take nine months to be born and another 15 or 16 years to grow up, and who really needs two grown-up, sensible parents who will make that new person welcome. But if one is very excited, or very anxious to see what love-making is like, it's easy to forget, or take a risk, or reckon it won't happen to you. Unfortunately girls don't have a bell which rings or a light which goes on when they have an ovum ready and sex will produce a baby. SO YOU MUST NEVER TAKE ANY CHANCES. Not even once.

Baby-making starts out of sight. All the time, the man is producing sperms.

Of the hundreds of millions of sperms in an ejaculate, only about 2,000 get to the place where the ovum is, and only one will actually fertilize it.

If the couple who are making love did not use any birth control (did not use any of the ways to make sure that a sperm and an ovum cannot meet, so that a baby cannot be produced), and if an ovum was ready in the woman's body, one of those 2,000 sperms may reach it, pierce its outer layer, leaving its long tail outside, and set the process of baby-making going. This is called "fertilization."

Actual baby-making begins when a couple starts to have intercourse unless they have taken precautions to prevent the woman from shedding an ovum, or to make sure that if she does the sperms cannot get to it.

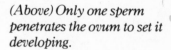

(Above) Only one sperm penetrates the ovum to set it developing.

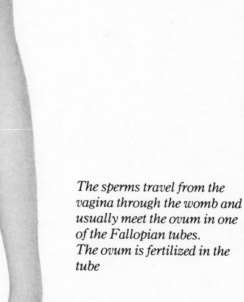

The sperms travel from the vagina through the womb and usually meet the ovum in one of the Fallopian tubes.
The ovum is fertilized in the tube

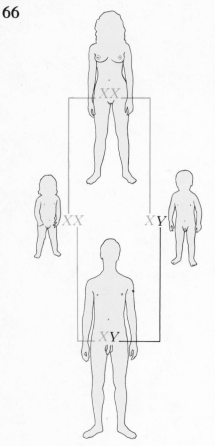

The instant that one sperm pierces the ovum wall, the wall itself changes with a click, and when this has happened, a second sperm cannot pierce it. Packed in the head of the successful sperm are half the chemical instructions for making a completely new person. The other half are in the ovum.

Inside the fertilized ovum the instructions from each parent pair up and combine. These "instructions" in cells which control their working are carried in sausage-shaped things called chromosomes. They determine, for example, what color our skin and hair will be. Every human cell has 23 pairs of chromosomes. Ovum and sperm each contain 23 single chromosomes, so each parent contributes half of the instructions in every cell. Every female cell has two identical small, or sex chromosomes (usually labeled by scientists with the letter X) while every male cell has two unlike sex chromosomes (labelled X and Y). There will be one sex chromosome in every ovum and one sex chromosome in every sperm. Since ova are only produced by women, and women have X + X in their cells, the ovum has no choice—its solitary sex chromosome has to be X. Sperms, however, are only produced by men, and men's cells have X + Y. The sex chromosomes in sperm can accordingly be either an X or a Y. In fact, sperms with an X and sperms with a Y are produced in about equal numbers. The result of this is obvious. If an X-bearing sperm gets to the ovum, X + X = XX, and the baby will be a girl. If a Y-bearing sperm gets there, X + Y = XY, and the baby will be a boy. Simple, but neat. It explains why boys and girls are born in roughly equal numbers.

If two ova are fertilized together, or if the ovum divides into two, the result will be twins. Twins from a single ovum are "identical" and, of course, they are of the same sex.

At first the fertilized ovum becomes a pinhead-sized ball of cells. It travels down into the uterus and burrows into the wall. As soon as this happens, chemical signals are sent to the other sex organs. The place in the ovary from which the ovum came turns into a hormone-producing organ which signals to the lining of the womb to develop, and turns off menstruation, so that the ovum doesn't get dumped along with the uterine lining. The whole womb increases in size. Before long the fertilized ovum has turned into an embryo, suspended in fluid and lying inside a globe of membranes. A blood system develops in it, and the place where the ovum first embedded turns into a special oxygen- and food-exchanging organ. The blood of the fetus does not mix with the blood of the mother, but the two run on opposite sides of a thin membrane system, so that the growing fetus can take food and oxygen from the mother's blood and pass out waste

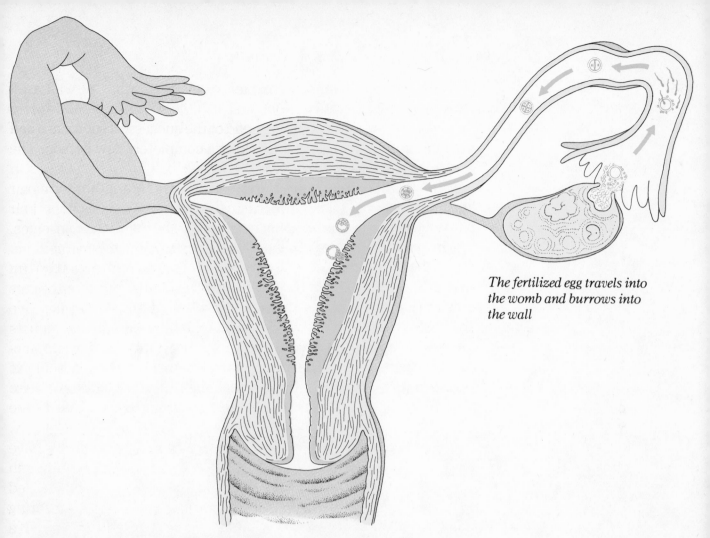

The fertilized egg travels into the womb and burrows into the wall

products for her kidneys to dispose of. This is the reason that a mother has to be careful what she takes in early pregnancy. Some drugs, and some germs, like the virus of German measles, can get through the membrane of the exchanger (which is called the placenta, Latin for "cake" because it looks like a pancake) and damage the growing fetus. The drug thalidomide, which caused many babies to be born abnormal when mothers took it in early pregnancy, was an example; recent work has shown that alcohol is nearly as dangerous, so a pregnant woman should avoid it. The baby's blood cannot actually mix with that of the mother, because it does not "match" with hers. Half of the baby's "instructions" come from the father, and if the placenta leaks, as it occasionally does, there may be trouble for future babies through a process rather like that of getting a wrongly matched blood transfusion. By the time the baby is ready to be born the pipes carrying blood to and from the placenta form a thick rope-like thing called the umbilical cord. It is very like the bundle of pipes and wires which joins an astronaut in space to his mother-spacecraft —which is called an umbilical for this reason. The growing fetus is in fact very like an astronaut, getting all the necessary support systems through pipes connecting it to the mother.

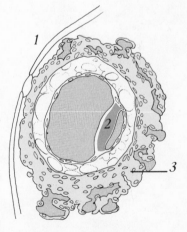

A section of a very early pregnancy embedded in the wall of the womb (1). (2) is the part which will develop into a baby. (3) is the area where the mother's and the baby's blood vessels come into contact. The other parts give rise to membranes in which the baby is enclosed

Our pictures show how the baby develops in the womb. Quite early on it is a tiny miniature person, complete with fingers and toes. At two months it is about an inch long. About the fifth month the mother can feel it moving inside her.

At the end of nine months the mother will have become quite large, and will have not only the baby but a bucket-full of fluid inside her which acts as packing. Finally she begins to notice cramp-like pains which show she is "going into labor." The cramps get stronger, the mouth of the uterus begins to pull open, and the membranes round the fetus break, letting out the fluid. Strong contractions of the womb then push the baby out, usually head-first and face-to-rear, down the vagina and out through the vulva. All the tissues are programmed to stretch without damage and let this happen. As soon as the baby's head is out, it can take its first breath. When this happens the arrangement of valves in its heart, which have so far kept blood from going through its lungs, because the mother's lungs have been breathing for it, snaps over to the "breathing" state. The blood

The growth of a baby in its mother's womb, month by month

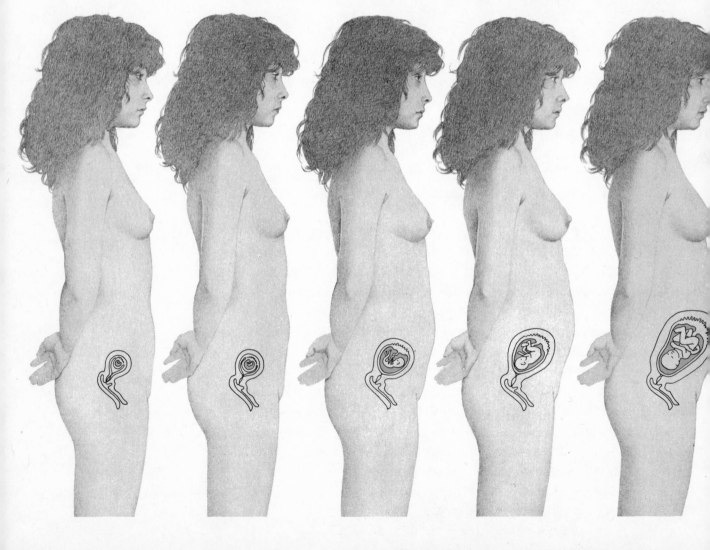

vessels from the exchanger, the placenta, which run to the baby's navel, are no longer needed. Usually the doctor or the nurse ties them and cuts the cord. The stump soon dries up and drops off a few days after birth—the "belly button" which we all have is the place where it used to be plugged in. Shortly after the baby is born, the placenta is jettisoned. In a few days the uterus goes back to its normal small size and before long the mother goes back to the shape she had before she was pregnant.

When a baby is born, you've made a baby—you haven't finished making a person. A baby pig can walk as soon as it is born: a human baby needs another 15 years at least of care from parents before it even approaches being "finished." The parents act like a second womb, and if they don't do their job properly the new person will suffer. One parent can bring up a child alone if necessary, and many do it excellently, but we are really programmed for two parents. Which is why you don't start baby-making on your own, or if you don't aim to finish it and produce a happy and fully made person at the end.

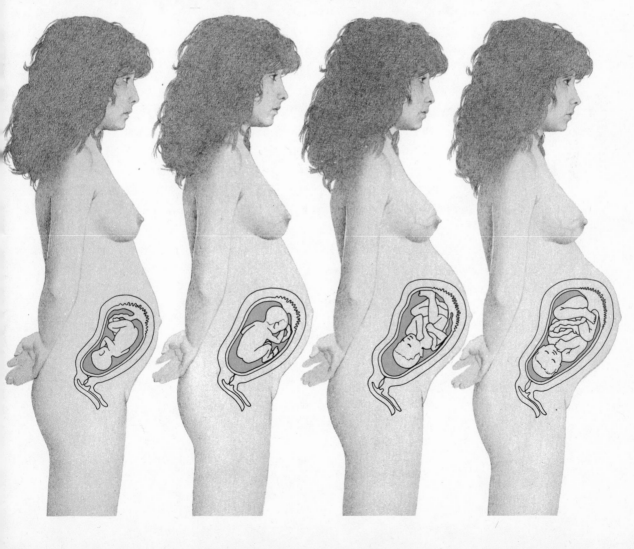

CONTRACEPTION

Birth control is probably the most important thing for young people to know about sex, because to enjoy sex and to make it part of caring, it is absolutely essential to be sure you won't produce a baby unless you want one. It's equally important for married people, so that they don't have more children than they really want, and every child they do have is a wanted child.

To have sex without babies you must stop the woman from shedding an ovum, or the man from making any sperms, or the sperms from getting to the ovum.

1 Sheath

Many people use the last of these ways. The easiest way to do this is for the man to put a thin rubber sheath (a "rubber," also called a condom) over the erect penis *before* he puts it anywhere near the vagina. These sheaths come rolled. You roll them on, a little like putting on a football sock. When the couple have had sex, the man must withdraw while he is still stiff. He must hold the sheath so that it does not pull off and stay behind. Sheaths are sold in drug stores. They come in little foil packs. They are quite a good way of preventing conception. But to make absolutely sure, in case the sheath were to tear or leak, the girl should *also* fill her vagina, before the man puts his penis in, with a special sperm-killing foam. This foam comes in special tubes and is squeezed in. How to do this is shown on the box. You have to be sure, if you have sex more than once, to put more foam in *before each* act. Sheaths and the little tubes of foam, which are not much bigger than a lipstick, are easy to carry in a purse. You need *both* a sheath and the special foam to be really safe. Soapsuds won't do instead of the special foam.

The sheath has to be put on the erect penis. This can be done while the woman is putting foam in her vagina. A new sheath must be used for every act of intercourse—they must not be used twice

2 Diaphragm

Women who are married, or are having intercourse often, may prefer to use a diaphragm. This is a rubber thing which is shaped a little like half an orange-skin. It is put into the vagina before having sex and covers the entrance to the womb. It has a sperm-killing jelly squeezed over it before it is put in. The woman leaves it in place for several hours after intercourse to make sure all the sperms are dead. Then she takes it out and washes it. Many married women use the diaphragm. It has to be fitted for you by a doctor or a nurse, to get the right size. The woman has to learn to put it in so that it is in the right place, and to check that she has done so. It is *not* safe to get hold of a diaphragm and put it in yourself for the first time: unless you have been taught how to use it, you will probably get pregnant. If you have been taught to use it and follow all the instructions carefully, it is a good method for many people.

3 IUD

Yet another way is for the doctor to put a small plastic or copper-coated gadget (called an IUD) not in the vagina but actually in the womb. The letters stand for "intra-uterine device." For some reason this acts to prevent an ovum from becoming embedded and developing. It can stay there quite a long time, as long as several months at a time, so the woman does not have to worry about precautions each time she has sex. It is a cheap way, but again it needs a doctor to put the device in place, and some women find they cannot use it.

(1) shows an IUD (a coil) in place, (2) a diaphragm in place, covering the entrance to the womb, (3) some of the most-used shapes of IUD, (4) a diaphragm

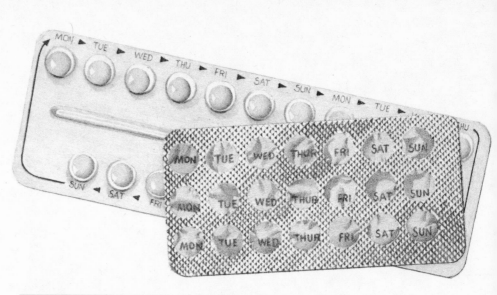

72 *Contraceptive pills come in packs which make it easy to remember to take them correctly. This picture shows two kinds of pack*

4 The Pill

The most certain way we have of preventing pregnancy is undoubtedly "the Pill." There are actually several different kinds of "Pill." They are still the subject of research, and they may not be the "best" form of birth control for everyone. The woman takes the pill either every day or on certain days of the month, according to the kind of pill she uses, and is prevented from shedding any ova, though she has periods as usual. She can take it for years, under medical supervision, then stop and have a child if she wants one. It needs a doctor's prescription, because some people should not use it for medical reasons, but if it is prescribed properly there is no reason to be afraid to use it. Even young girls can get it from many doctors without having to tell anyone else. If the Pill is taken exactly as directed it is 100 percent effective in preventing conception.

There is more than one kind of Pill; you must follow the instructions to the letter. You may have read that taking the Pill can cause complications—if your doctor has prescribed it for you, you need not worry, however. Many of the complications affect older women, especially if they also smoke cigarettes.

For the contraceptive Pill to work it has to be taken all the time, exactly as directed, even if you are not having sex with anyone just then. Young girls who get some birth control pills belonging to someone else and take one or two of them, thinking that this will prevent them having a baby, are not protected at all. It usually takes a month, or one menstrual cycle, for the doctor to check that the Pill is working. So it is *not* a method you can use by yourself. Foam and the sheath used together are really the only kind of birth control young people can use successfully without getting adult help. If you are going to have sex, you MUST use one or another of these methods.

Sticking to the Rules

Methods that don't work, and that you should never rely on, are the trick of counting up days to see when the woman should shed an ovum, and only having sex at other times (the "safe period"), putting things like lemon juice in the vagina, washing out the vagina after sex, and trying to pull out the penis just before the sperm is discharged. People who use these methods end up as—parents.

If you do have sex without precautions, either because you were forced to, or because something went wrong, like a sheath splitting when you didn't use foam as well, see a doctor at once, to make sure you don't get pregnant. If you did become pregnant, it would be possible early on to stop the pregnancy by taking out the developing ovum, but this needs an operation ("abortion"), and though this might be better than having a baby you don't intend to, or can't, care for properly, it would never be needed if people took proper precautions. On no account do anything yourself, or let anyone else who isn't a doctor do anything to "get rid" of a pregnancy—this will not work, and could easily kill you.

People who are quite sure they will never want, or never again want, to have a child, can be made safe against conceiving or fathering a baby—the man by having the tubes which carry the sperm tied (vasectomy) the woman by having the same thing done to the tubes which carry the ova (sterilization or "tubal ligation"). Doctors don't like doing these operations in young people who might come to change their minds later and want to be parents. The changes are meant to be permanent—they can sometimes be reversed, but one can't rely on this.

All but one of the birth control methods (the sheath) which young people commonly use are things which the woman has to see to. This seems a bit unfair. Probably one day there will be a pill which the man can take—at present there isn't a good one. His part is to make absolutely sure that both he himself and the woman have taken precautions, before he puts his penis anywhere near her vulva, and to use a sheath and foam if she hasn't or doesn't seem sure. Lying to a sexual partner about whether you have taken precautions is a frightful and cruel thing to do. So is having sex without bothering about precautions.

The trouble about some methods is that you don't always know when you will want to have sex. If a girl is on the Pill, she does not have to plan in advance. The sheath and foam are things the boy or girl can easily carry around in a purse or pocket.

74

The "best" method of birth control is the one which gives the most protection against having an unwanted baby and which most people can use. All of the methods we have given are used by some people. A clinic or a doctor can help you choose yours when the time comes for you to have sex. For young people who are beginning sex, the surest method is the Pill, unless there are medical reasons why the girl cannot take it; the next best is the sheath plus foam. If the sheath is used by the boy *and* a contraceptive foam by the girl, they will have very good protection, and both of these are easy methods which are always ready—the Pill has to be taken all of the time, even when the girl is not going to have sex just then. Also, both the sheath and the foam can be bought without any prescription, and if you use both of them, *both* partners are showing they are fit to have sex by taking responsible precautions.

Many people get pregnant through having sex when they've been drinking, which can make them want sex, but also makes them muddled or careless. Good sex and drink or drugs don't mix.

You can get just as pregnant the very first time you have sex as at any other time. So the rule is—birth control comes first. No exceptions. No excuses.

The best way to make sure of birth control which works is to get advice from a doctor or a clinic

When you are ready to have sex—which will be when you are mature and old enough to handle this important thing sensibly and well, you must FIND OUT ABOUT BIRTH CONTROL BEFORE YOU EVEN TRY TO HAVE INTERCOURSE, find out EXACTLY how to use whatever method you are going to use, and MAKE SURE YOU USE IT CORRECTLY.

If you use the sheath by itself and don't take care in using it that the sperm doesn't leak out, or if you are on the Pill and don't remember to take it exactly as the doctor orders (there are always instructions on the pack, and the individual pills are usually packed in a way which helps you to remember) the method won't work.

Your parents, a counselor, a birth control clinic, or a doctor, can tell you how to do these things. DON'T get your information from other boys and girls at school or elsewhere: what they think they know may be wrong.

If you don't GET IT RIGHT, there is always the risk of starting a pregnancy.

VIRGINS

A "virgin" is simply somebody who never had sex with anyone. It used to be thought that you could tell if a girl was a virgin by looking at her sex organs—you can't. The little skin tag across the vagina called the "hymen" or maidenhead may get torn the first time she has sex, but it often doesn't, and it can be torn in other ways, so there is no way of telling. Since there is a first time for everything, every boy and every girl is a virgin to start with.

People often forget that boys as well as girls start life as virgins—usually the word is used about the girl.

Many people have felt, and still feel, that being a virgin is in some way special. It is easy to see why this is so—with something which is as important as sexuality, the first time is indeed important.

Any person may be a little shy the first time he or she has sex, boys quite as much as girls. You should always ask, and go extra gently if they are first-timers, so as to help them. Having a bad first experience can spoil things badly for both boys and girls and make them not enjoy sex later on.

If it's your partner's first time but not yours, help your partner to learn and be patient. If it's the first time for both of you, be gentle and you'll both learn to enjoy it. There is no reason for the girl to be afraid that she will be hurt.

The notion that it's big or manly to be the first male to have sex with a lot of girls, and then drop them, is silly behavior which hurts them and only makes you look like a heel. People need a first experience with someone who cares how they feel, not a clown who merely wants to "have their cherry" as if he were collecting stamps.

Many young people who have read or heard that sex is something terrific are pretty much disappointed the first time they have it. Sometimes the boy finds that he gets so anxious that he cannot get an erection at all, or that he ejaculates almost before starting to have intercourse. Instead of feeling like a space shot launch, nothing much happens. Aside from the fact that they are often nervous, or a bit anxious whether they are doing right, or scared that adults will find out and be angry, or that they won't know what to do, it's not surprising. Sex has to be learned, and you have to get comfortable with it to enjoy it properly.

The first time you ski, or go to a dance, or pitch at baseball isn't usually the time you enjoy it most. It can go like a bomb the very first time with any of these, and so it can with sex. But it often doesn't—so don't worry.

NONSENSES

Although having sex is one of the most enjoyable things we do, generations of people have made themselves and others miserable by worrying, preaching about it, prohibiting it, and writing nonsense about it. Why this has been so, we simply don't know. Partly, as we've said, it was because of the risk of pregnancy. But quite apart from this, in every generation a few people have gone around claiming that sex was sinful, harmful, dangerous, shameful, and to be avoided. People have often listened to them and believed them. If you show a normal human body on a public beach by swimming without a swimsuit you can still get arrested as a "sex criminal." Not long ago there were men who went through life without ever seeing a naked woman, and women who never saw a naked man, because husbands and wives thought it "not nice" to undress in front of each other. Even copies of Greek statues had the relevant parts left out or covered up. Married people often only had sex in the dark, wearing nightshirts.

You are incredibly lucky in being the first generation to have the chance of being free of this kind of nonsense. You will have to cope with some of the leftovers, such as silly laws, or people who are still anxious and upset if they suspect that you are enjoying sexuality. One reason for this new freedom is the fact that for the first time it is possible if you act responsibly to have sex in the certainty that you won't also have a baby; in the past, that risk was always present. Another reason is the growth of knowledge. For years people repeated and believed nonsense about sex—that masturbation was harmful, for example, or that for a woman to kiss a man's penis or a man a woman's vulva was "perverted." It was only when scientists started to collect the facts—and found that nearly everyone enjoys these things—that the nonsenses could be put down. We haven't talked much here about nonsenses, except where we needed to tell you that they aren't true, but you will hear plenty of them. So it is even more important to get your facts right about sex than about anything else.

People are now less inclined to pretend about sex than they were in the past. Some people in the past did all of the things people do now. The difference is that now they talk frankly about them and don't believe so many wrong statements. Accordingly, you will be freer in a sense to enjoy sex because you will know more and not be worried by nonsense. At the same time, you will have to grow up faster and learn the needs of other people earlier, because the responsibility for treating your sexuality rightly will be yours. When boys and girls did not know the facts, they were kept apart and punished if they experimented. It was in a sense easier even if many of the rules were silly. Being free means being sensible, knowing the facts, and not doing things which hurt other people—otherwise you don't deserve the freedom you have.

Here are a few common false beliefs:

—masturbation makes you sick or pimply

—a girl can get pregnant from being kissed, or kissing a boy's penis, or swallowing semen

—you can't get pregnant unless you "come"

—a man can't have sex twice in one day

—it's dangerous to have sex during a period

—you shouldn't swim or bathe during a period

—having sex with everyone in sight is a way of proving you are an attractive person

—you can't get pregnant if you hold your breath when the man comes

—people over 40, or 50, or 60, or 70, can't have sex any more

—marrying and having babies is the proper ambition for every girl, and if you don't there is something wrong with you

—sex is a kind of Olympic contest, in which you need to perform

—balling every girl who will stay still is evidence of great masculinity

—pictures of sex and sex acts are nasty, disgusting, and a cause of crime

—the only proper use of sex is to make babies—using it for pleasure is "lust"

—there are drugs, foods or other things you take ("aphrodisiacs") that can make you sexually excited

—all men want a lot of sexual partners; all women want one true love

Every one of these should be marked "wrong"—it simply is not true.

THE SEXUAL REVOLUTION?

You sometimes hear about a "sexual revolution"—meaning that people's ideas about sex, and the rules they make about it, have changed a great deal.

The really big change is that science has now made it possible to have sex and be sure that it won't produce a baby. Until very recently the risk was always there. Obviously, while this was so, boys and girls, or men and women, couldn't ever treat sex as play, or even risk having it at all before they were married; though they often did, and it often did produce unwanted babies. You can see why the rules were so very strict. But those rules can only be changed if people use the methods which have been found to stop unwanted pregnancies and use them properly and every time. Otherwise the old rules still apply. Yet a lot of young people refuse to follow the old rules (they have sex just when they want to) but don't follow the new rule, that all this freedom depends on proper birth control. In America every year a million, or one in ten, teenage girls get pregnant, often while they are still children or still at school—which means that about a million boys the same age didn't bother either. Some of these will be married, and some will get married because they are pregnant, but you don't want to become a statistic, and you have no right to start something you can't finish. Either understand the new rules, or stick to the old ones—no sex until you are married and able to raise a family. It's as simple as that. Freedom never means being free to be selfish, silly and careless. Nobody who doesn't understand this and stick to it is grown-up enough to have sexual intercourse with another person.

RELIGIONS, RULES & SEX

Many religions have made rules governing sexual behavior. The rules embodied in the Jewish religion are set forth in the Old Testament. Christianity has adopted many of these rules, and different Christian believers have added others in accordance with their beliefs and the teaching of their Churches. Moslem rules of conduct are set out in the Koran.

Rules often take the line that some kinds of sexual act are always wrong and to be avoided, and those who practice the religions which make these rules guide their conduct by them.

Other religious thinkers believe that whether an act is good or bad often depends upon the thinking behind it, and that what matters in sexual behavior is that our actions ought to be guided by care, concern and love for other people. In some cases the religious view of a particular sex act has changed as we have come to know more about human sexual behavior. Yet other rules come not from religious teaching but from what people in a particular age think "respectable"—rules against talking about sexuality or seeing the naked human body have often been of this kind. Rules like these change greatly from time to time.

All people have the right to choose the rules by which they will live, just as they have the right to choose whether they will follow a particular religion. Nearly everyone agrees that selfish, unloving sexual behavior is bad, however—and also that it is much less enjoyable than being caring toward others. This applies not only to sex behavior but to living generally.

The truth is that people are different, have different needs, and live differently. Some people do indeed have sex with only one partner all their lives, and prefer it that way—others don't. Some people enjoy very varied sex play, others don't. It is fairly easy to know what you think you like, though you may change that view when you try it or as you get older. Since sex involves two people most of the time, you also have to find out what your partner thinks and needs.

Learning to find out and meet the needs of another person and also your own needs is probably the most important thing young people gain from sexual experience. Which is why selfishly doing your own thing, on the one hand, and setting strict rules for yourself which go against your own common sense, on the other, are both bars to growing into caring, responsible, adults.

You live in a country where you will meet people who have many different religious beliefs, so you can't guess what they believe to be right and wrong in sexual behavior. If you yourself have been brought up in a particular faith you will know, or you can easily find out, what rules of sexual conduct it teaches. There are also many people who do not have any very strong belief in a religious system of conduct. If you are one of these people, it can be difficult to realize that people who think otherwise can also have good and enjoyable sex lives by following the rules which they have learned, from the Bible, from the Torah, from the church to which they belong. Sex is not something you keep in a watertight box—the way each of us uses it is part of our whole way of looking at life. If it doesn't fit with our other attitudes, with our beliefs about what is important and right, we are not likely to get the best out of it. Religious faith is one way that people try to get a clear pattern in their lives—if they see a different pattern from yours, you must respect that.

GOING WITH THE CROWD

One thing we need to learn is to be tolerant of other folk's sex needs without feeling pressured to imitate them. Among young people, the ones that "do it" often reckon the ones that "don't do it" are squares. The ones that "don't" reckon the ones that "do" are tramps. Usually neither group knows what the other really does—only what they say

they do. There is only one good reason for joining in any kind of sexual activity—that you feel it is right for you at that particular time with that particular person—and you are fully able to handle it responsibly. People who have strong religious or moral beliefs would be quite wrong to do things they do not feel comfortable with, simply because others don't feel the same. Do what's right for *you*. Being scared into sex and being scared out of sex are neither of them good ways of choosing how you will behave.

HOMOSEXUALITY

Not only are boys sexually attractive to girls, and girls to boys: all young humans are to some extent sexually attractive to each other and like looking at and touching each other. A pair of boys may masturbate together, and some then go on to masturbate each other. Some girls do the same—or youngsters may "fall in love" with an attractive older person (often called "having a crush") who may be of the same sex. This is all a normal part of development. After puberty most people concentrate their sexual interest on the other sex, and our society has always trodden very hard on those who went on showing sexual interest in people of their own sex—boys more than girls, because fathers thought that for a boy to love a boy was perverted and meant that he was unmanly and a queer. People who still found members of their own sex attractive sexually were jailed, executed, tortured, and generally treated as criminals. This is odd, because in some societies it was thought quite natural for boys and men, or women and girls, to have sex together, either as a change, or

for special reasons (a Greek hero with his shieldbearer, for instance) or because they preferred it. People who prefer to make love to a person of their own sex are called homosexual (*homo-* means "same") or very often "gay." Women who prefer other women to men are sometimes called "Lesbians." "Gay Liberation," which you may read about, means the idea that these people have a right to choose whom they love without being kicked around by other people because of it. Why some people find it more pleasant to have sex with their own sex we don't know. People who *only* are attracted to their own sex are much fewer than those who are attracted to the other sex. They are *not* sick or abnormal—they just have different tastes.

If we weren't brought up with such strict rules about how men and women were expected to behave, most of us would probably come somewhere between wanting only other-sex and only wanting same-sex contacts, with rather more people who prefer other-sex. People who know that they enjoy both are called "bisexuals." Probably the ability to love anybody, of either sex, physically, given suitable circumstances, is natural to humans anyway, though our society doesn't encourage it.

In any big group of people, there will be some who have sex with people of their own sex. You can't pick them out by looking at them

In homosexual sex, people make love by kissing and masturbating each other. Men also sometimes put the penis in the back passage as if it were a vagina and have intercourse this way. If young people play sex games with their own sex this doesn't mean they are homosexual. Nor does having homosexual fantasies or dreams—nearly everyone has these. It's a bad idea to get stuck too early with the idea you are "homosexual" because you had some sex with a person of your own sex.

It would be a great pity to miss out on sex with the other sex if that is something you could enjoy. It is not true that homosexuals are people who go around assaulting children, any more than other-sex-inclined (or "straight") adults do. But it's certainly wise to avoid much older folk of either sex who make sex advances to you when you are still growing up: they are often people with serious problems.

It's also untrue that you can tell if people are "gay" by looking at them. Some husky footballers have sex only with other men: most long-haired male musicians have sex only with girls. And the same applies to women who prefer other women. Gay people have had a lot of problems from the bad way society treats them. You don't need to add to these.

Now that there is a lot of talk about homosexuality, young people who are anxious about growing up very often worry about it. If they find people of their own sex attractive, or even have played some sexual games with someone of their own sex, or have been persuaded to do so by an older person, the pressure is on to assume that they have found what will be their pattern for life. This may upset them a lot, and may actually stop them finding out whether they like other-sex relations as much or more. If, like many young people, they are a little bit scared of the other sex and are anxious in case they aren't found attractive themselves, they can "get stuck" with a style which doesn't really suit them and can make them unhappy.

If you ever run into this kind of problem, talk about it to a counselor whom you can trust. Although some people do indeed find that they prefer all their lives to have sex with people of their own sex, one can't know this until one is fully grown up. In spite of a lot which you will see written, people who are really quite unable to relate sexually to the other sex are rather rare,—many who think they can't have made up their minds too soon that they couldn't.

As with all other parts of growing up, this is a clear case where you should take your time, and get advice from somebody skilled and sensible if you need it. There is a chapter on "getting help" further on in this book.

NAKEDNESS

It's too bad that we are taught to be ashamed of the naked body. Being naked both feels good and looks good—in fact even ugly people often look better, not worse, with no clothes on.

Stopping people from being naked (on beaches, for example) or from seeing other people naked, is an industry, which employs hundreds of policemen, inspectors, district attorneys and so on. It seems rather silly.

People who found out that it really felt good to be naked together in the open air in order to play games, swim and tan used to be called "nudists." Taking off your clothes in company means seeing other people as they are, letting them see you as you are, without any cover-up, and is reassuring for anyone who wonders how he or she rates physically as a man or woman. They learn that people are of all shapes and sizes, and all shapes and sizes look good, with or without clothes.

Many adults now walk around naked at home and don't hide behind towels. This helps children to know what adult bodies look like. Some men grew up in the last century without knowing that women have hair around their sex parts—pictures and statues used to leave it out—and were quite upset when they found what naked women really look like; many girls didn't know till they were married how big a normal penis is.

In our lifetime people will probably stop making such a fuss over nakedness. At the moment you have to remember that it still upsets some people, rather as sex in general upsets some people, and it isn't particularly considerate to make these people look at it if they don't want to.

"Nudists" used to make a big thing of lying about in the sun getting browned all over, and claimed that it was this that made them feel good. Probably it was really the fact of getting rid of all the old nonsense about nakedness being dirty or shameful which made them feel good. It is pleasant to lie in the sun, and brown skin looks healthy—but actually sunlight damages the skin and makes it wrinkle early, so it is better not to get too much of it, particularly in very sunny places like Florida and California, or at the top of mountains, where the sun is strong.

Being naked together is one of the pleasantest things lovers do, even when they aren't going to have sex. It lets them see and feel each other without hiding anything, simply as two complete people.

One thing the "dirty" notion of nakedness has managed to do is

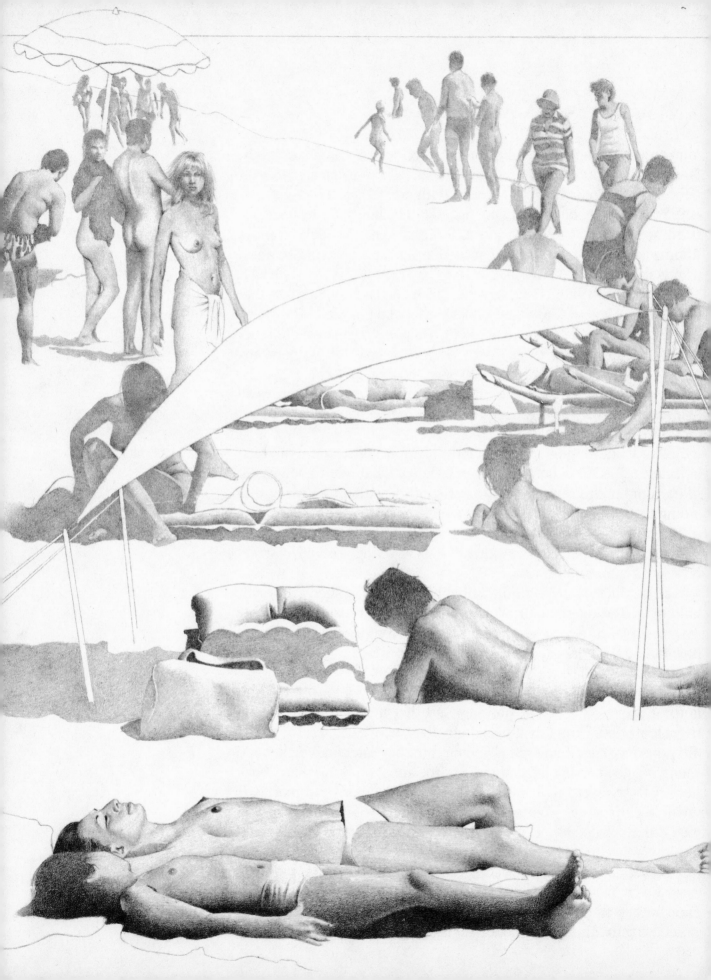

manufacture an actual illness. Some men, who have had sex difficulties since childhood and are too scared inside to have proper sex with a woman, are only "turned on" by hiding around in public places and suddenly showing their sex organs to a woman or a young girl. If she is shocked and shows it, they feel good. These people are called "exhibitionists" or flashers, and are often sent to jail. One should be sorry they have such problems, but they don't actually hurt anyone. If all women and girls were used to looking at a normal male body, they would do what one French lady is said to have done, and say to the man "Great, but won't you catch cold like that?"

WHAT SEX IS FOR:
2 Love

People often say that what matters is not "sex" but love, and that sex without loving the person you have sex with is not good. The word "love" is used in many ways. You can love your mother, love your country, or love baseball, and being "in love" usually refers to the special attraction between two people, when they want to be together a lot, and probably want to have sex together. Young people who are going together often ask each other "Do you really love me?"

The best way to explain what sort of "love" there has to be between people to make sex something great for both of them is to say that two people love each other when they like and care for each other just as they find each other. They want to please each other and share with each other. They are comfortable together, and want to be absolutely sure that each gives the other something good and special, not bad feelings afterward. This could happen in quite different ways. One couple could feel all these things and want each other so much that they might feel they needed to be always together, and perhaps spend their lives together and have children. Another couple might only know that just now they were both quite happy together, enjoying one another, and ready to see how much more there was to know about one another. We would call both of these love. The important thing in real love is feeling happy with a person just as he or she is, not wanting to change, pressure or own them, because they are people, and you can't "own" a person—and knowing they feel the same about you. People in real life don't always wait to have sex until they feel as good as this about one another. Sometimes they need to have sex to learn that much about each other. But to have sex at all you've at least got to have *caring*, or it will turn into something unkind which both people will feel badly about later.

90 *Love means wanting to be together and . . .*

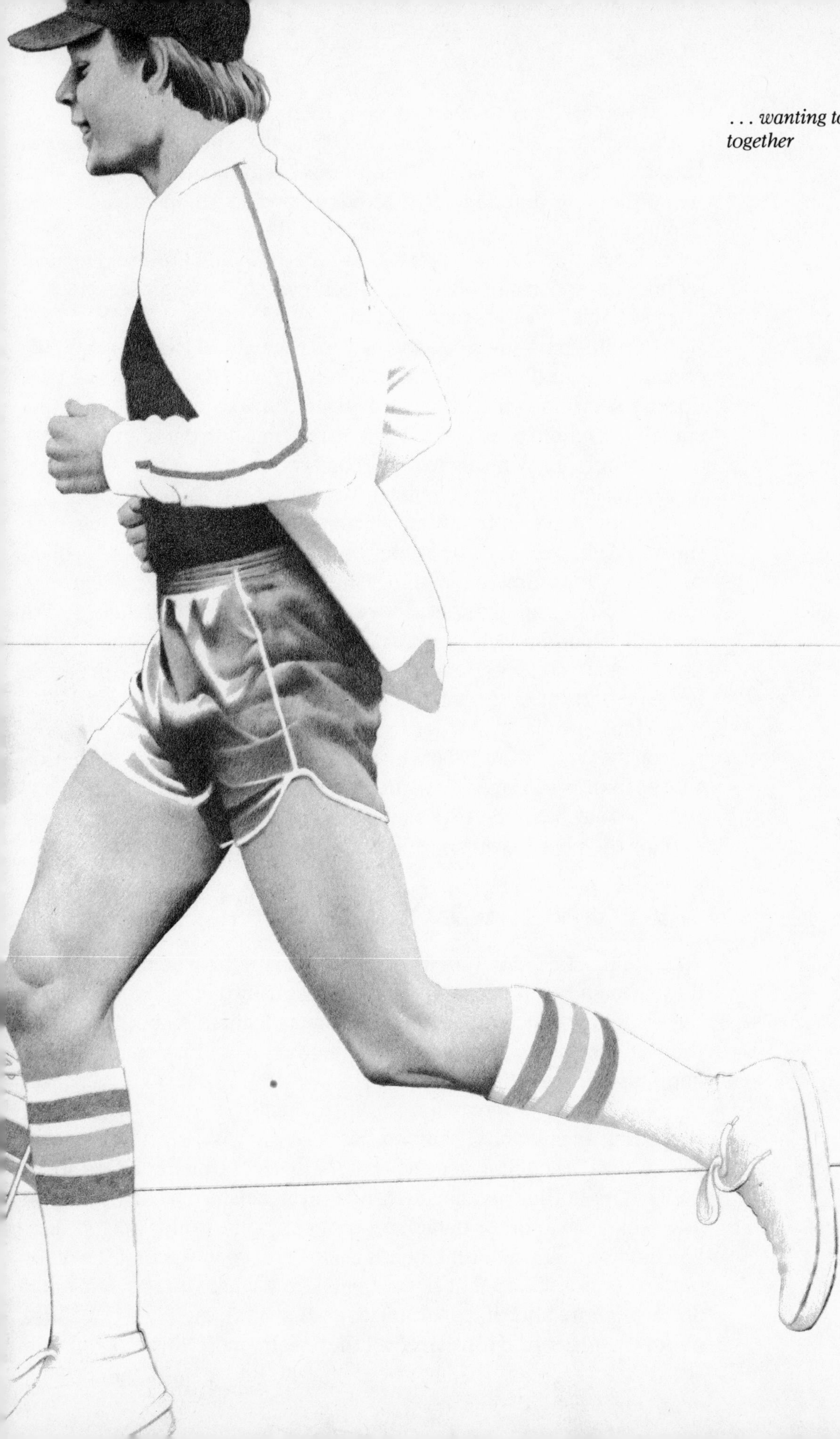

If you are very excited sexually by somebody and want to have sex with them, it's a temptation to pretend you like them more than you do. This is an unkind thing to do, because it leaves the other person feeling dumped or rejected, when they thought you cared about them. If two people both feel excited and want sex together, there is nothing wrong with that, but they shouldn't pretend to have feelings they don't really have. If you have to *persuade* someone to have sex with you, it's usually better not to have it.

People sometimes argue whether it is natural to be jealous. It's certainly natural to be hurt if someone whom one loves very much doesn't seem to return that love. It's natural to be afraid of losing somebody whom one loves. At the same time one cannot try to own another person. Wanting to own somebody as if he or she were a pet or a bicycle isn't really a loving attitude.

People have difficulty at all ages in dealing with feelings like these. When one is starting to form relationships with other young people it's important to remember that both you and they are learning. Even if you like another person very much, both you and they need to go out with others and perhaps fall in love with others: beside, you don't need to do everything in pairs, and you need to mix with people *not* on a partner or lover basis.

Many people decide far too soon that they have found the only person they ever want to be with or have sex with, which is one reason that so many marriages break up. Because feelings are so strong, it is hard to treat your first experiences as a learning period, both for you and for the people you share it with—but that is what it is.

MANNERS & MORALS

When adults talk about "morals," or about something being "immoral," they're usually talking about sex. Morals really means right conduct, but somehow people have always made a bigger fuss about sex rules than about things like greed or prejudice or failure to care what happens to others.

We think there are only two "moral" sex rules—don't risk producing an unwanted baby, and don't do things which hurt someone else. Most of the other sex rules people learn in growing up are about how to treat other people and are really sex *manners*. Any time you have sex with another person, even if you both want it only for fun, you have to be *caring*; that means that you have to see that the other person enjoys it too, that both of you know what you are doing and don't get hurt and disappointed, and that both have good feelings about it afterward. However cool they seem, most young people are pretty uncertain when they start having sex. They're afraid the other person won't find them terrific, that they will be put down, that other people look better or are more manly or more experienced or have nicer hair or breasts. And so on.

Manners mean putting your partner at ease, not saying things which could hurt them, like "Why do you have those pimples?" or "Gee, what a little cock (or what little breasts) you have." Manners mean not rushing off afterward, but staying and saying thank you; they just did something good for you, so thank them, even though you just did something good for them. Manners mean not being so hell-bent on sex that you talk someone into having it who doesn't want it, or into staying out late so that parents are upset, and not boasting to others when you have had sex with someone.

Manners mean not teasing people and making them sexually excited when you don't intend to have sex with them at all. Manners mean keeping joshing and fooling under control. It may be fun to whistle at an attractive person, and for that person to pretend to be mad about it if you do, but some people resent it—girls particularly, because there is a long history of mean treating women like goods in a supermarket. This is now out of date and offensive. In any case whistling at people or pinching them isn't a good way of making friends—caring and frankness are.

When young people start looking for sex experience they nearly all think you have to be handsome or beautiful and that they aren't. One thing they learn is that caring scores much higher. Take a look at the grown-up lovers you know—if people had to be "beautiful" to make out, half of them would still be way down the field. All people are lovable whatever shape they are, and even if they have a problem such as a disability or spots. The only exceptions are the stinkers who are interested only in themselves and in scoring. These people are heels, whether male or female. Manners mean you care about the other person, as a part of your own enjoyment.

One trouble young folk often have is that they don't know much about each other's reactions. Boys (and some girls) can be heavy-handed and clumsy in touching the other sex. Because a girl feels good when her breasts or her clitoris are touched, that doesn't mean she will feel better still if you squeeze them hard. Boys are inclined to hurry, and to be set on getting that penis in. If the girl isn't ready, having it pushed in will hurt. Girls are inclined not to realize how fast a boy can turn on. A few kisses and the sight of a nice pair of breasts, or even a girl's underclothes, can do the trick; then the girl may be scared, and want to turn off. Boys can get a girl equally aroused by "heavy petting" and leave her high and dry in the same way. People who do this get a bad name as teasers.

If you do find you've excited someone but you don't want to go all the way—either because you just don't choose to, or because you know you aren't safe against getting pregnant, tell the other person gently (and as soon as you see they *are* getting excited) and ask if there is any other way you can release the tension. Anyone can give another person a climax by hand or in some other way which doesn't involve intercourse. You don't have to take risks in order to be considerate.

WHEN?

Some people believe young folk should not be told all about sex because if they read about it, know how it is done, and realize how pleasant it is, they will start doing it while they are still children and cause themselves all kinds of bad trouble.

Many young people do start having sexual intercourse far too young, getting pregnant, letting sex interfere with their schoolwork, and giving themselves and their parents a lot of heartache.

We think that if you have taken the trouble to read so far and found it interesting, you will see *why* it is silly to rush things. Seeing why, we think, is more likely to make you think twice and wait a while than simply saying "don't." Sexual intercourse is for men and women, not children.

When should a person start having sex? The law fixes this age, but the age varies from state to state, and has ranged from 12 to 21 in different states at different times. Boys have to be careful to observe these laws, or they can get into serious trouble. The real answer is "not until they want to and are fully ready to handle it." It's very difficult for you—or anyone else—to be sure when this is, and it is harder for girls than for boys, because often they are in two minds about sex until they are quite adult. They may be under pressure from boys, as well as from needs of their own they don't entirely understand. At least "being ready" would have to include being ready and willing to take proper birth control precautions, and taking them.

All people begin to have sex before they know *all* about it, or about how to treat other people. This is because sex is like mountain climbing: you can learn the basics, and how to avoid dangers, before you start, but in the end you have to learn by doing it. The same applies to all relations between people. Sometimes you get bruises, but you learn. The main thing is to try to avoid giving a hard time to anyone else, whether that is a partner, a parent or a baby whom you might have—and you don't want to give yourself a hard time either.

It used to be thought wrong ever to have sex before you are married. Before there was birth control, this was true. Some people believe that it still is, and are more comfortable waiting until after marriage. Don't ever hassle a person who feels this way to have sex because *you* want it. When to have sex and when to say no are things people have an absolute right to choose for themselves.

Other people say that since marriage means promising to try to live with a person always, it's silly to promise until you know that person really well, which includes knowing if you please one another sexually and can make one another feel really good. One can be misled over this by the fact that it often takes several years for two people to "get it on," but the idea makes sense. Many young people who have intercourse before marriage do so only with one or two other people, and then marry one of those people. Others have sex

People never get too old for love and sex

98

with a lot of people—every person has different needs. If you have sex with a huge number of people it gets hard to be really caring about them. Often people who do this are scared that they aren't lovable, and have to keep proving that they are, which isn't much fun.

The important thing is to have sex only when it's "right" for you, with a partner who feels it's "right"—whether you love each other a lot, or whether it's just play between you. Don't ever be pressured into sex because you want to be liked, or because "everyone in our class" says they have it, or with a person you aren't comfortable with. People boast a lot about things they'd like to do, or they think other people would admire them for doing. The Tiggers who rush around being studs or campus punch-boards, or saying how many people they had sex with, often are less sexual people than the Pooh types who don't say so much.

Remember also that *there is plenty of time*. One can feel at 14 like an old man or an old woman who isn't ever going to make it with anyone. At 14, people find it very hard to realize that at 25 or 30 they'll wonder why there was such a hurry. Being worried that you aren't liked, or feeling rushed, only makes it harder to get to know other people.

Lastly, however anxious adults have been and are about sex, don't be scared of it. In any worthwhile undertaking, whether it's sex or climbing, one may take tumbles or even get hurt. Being sensible and careful and considerate doesn't mean being scared. It helps to avoid being badly hurt or hurting others. The people who are in real trouble are the people who are so scared that they miss the whole reward of taking part. These people need help to be less scared. We've written in another part of this book about where people can get this kind of help (p. 111). If you do have worries there is no reason why you should have to deal with them all by yourself.

One good thing about sex is that it will almost certainly last as long as you do. Young people often think that nobody over 50 can possibly be having sex, or enjoying it if they do. In fact, people who are well go on having sex until they are 70, 80 or 90. No man ever stopped being able to get erections, and no woman ever stopped enjoying orgasm, just because they were old. When they do stop, it's because they have become ill or infirm, or have no partner and can't find one, or because people have cruelly led them to think that for older people to have sex is "not nice." In fact—though it's hard to believe this when you are young—sex gets better as you get older and more experienced. You should hope that your grandparents are still enjoying it as much as you do, and that when you are their age you'll enjoy it as much as they do.

PARENTS

Young people often complain that "they can't talk to their parents" or that "adults don't understand." It isn't always obvious while one is young that adults, including parents, often can and would help, that talking to them might make things a lot easier, and that using their love for you and their experience of life is what parents are about.

If you ever have children, you will understand why parents try to keep young people out of trouble, want them to share the ideas, the religious opinions, and the knowledge which they themselves have found helpful, and are worried that things may go wrong. Some of the things that look quite simple and obvious when one is fourteen or fifteen look a lot more complicated when one has lived another ten or fifteen years.

Parents are basically concerned that you shouldn't hurt yourself. They also have grown up themselves, before you did, and have had to find ways of handling things you will have to handle.

These are some good ways *not* to talk to parents: to start by assuming they "don't understand" what you feel at your age; or that it will "blow their minds" if they do; to reckon that because they have ways of doing things, or ideas, which you've often heard them recommend, those ways must automatically be "old hat" and no use to you; and to quote at them things other people say, including things in this book, which you know or suspect they wouldn't agree with, in a down-putting way. Nobody likes being knocked, any more than you do yourself. Good ways to talk to them are to be frank, to ask questions about what you hear and read, and to listen when you get answers. How humans should live, including how they should manage their sex lives, is a difficult question, and has more than one answer. In reading a book, you are learning what the people who wrote it believe. If you talk about what we have written and hear what other people think, including first of all your parents, it will do more good than treating what you read as necessarily the whole truth. These are matters about which different people have different views.

Not only youngsters but many people who are grown up, find it quite difficult to talk about sex. Grown-up people may find it more difficult than you do, because they have lived longer than you and realize what a complicated set of questions it raises. Not everyone is going to be able to give you a lecture on biology, and nobody wants to be put through a quiz, particularly if you are really not asking straight questions but prying or asking "did you always do exactly as you're telling me to do?" or "didn't you ever make mistakes?" Very loving

parents usually find it really difficult to know just what they ought to say to their children about sex and how they ought to say it. One point of having this book is to provide a kind of bridge. Obviously, if your parents gave it to you you can ask them about it. If you got it elsewhere, you could still ask them to read it and tell you what they think themselves.

All young folk, including your parents when they were young, need much the same questions answered. All young folk like different clothes and music from their parents, at least for a while, and tend to assume that older people couldn't possibly understand what it is like to be young. It's well worth trying hard to see whether or not they can!

If you really can't talk to parents, or they aren't around for any reason, choose a sensible adult, like a school counselor or teacher or a doctor you like. Of course you can and probably will talk to people your own age or a little older, but don't assume that they know the answers, however sure they sound. Sometimes there really is no substitute for adults. Adults, especially parents, are there to help you; their concern is to try and give you the best advice.

Parents have often been through the same problems that worry their children. Caring parents are one of the best sources of advice

WHAT SEX IS FOR:
3 Fun

Beside all the other uses, sex is *play*. You can play any game you both enjoy. Some people have worried themselves sick whether the games they enjoy playing are "unnatural," "perverted" and so on. Anything two lovers do is natural, provided they both enjoy it and it isn't quite obviously silly and dangerous, like hurting one another. Some people have worried that it was "unnatural" to masturbate, or to masturbate each other—to kiss each other's sex organs, for the girl to come on top instead of underneath, for people to dress up, or play pretend-games—in fact, just about everything except quick sex with him on top and her underneath.

The rule is—lovers should do anything they both enjoy. Each must find out what his or her partner would enjoy trying and do that: no one should ever force any sort of sex play on anyone; they should use exactly the kind of common sense they'd use in playing any other pretend game to avoid doing anything which is painful, dangerous or off-putting. One must learn to meet the other person's needs—some like their sex very gentle, with a lot of skin touching. People like different parts of their body, not only their sex organs, kissed touched, fondled and massaged. Often they'll tell you which. If they don't know, good lovers see if the two of them can find out what

Love and marriage are serious, but loving people spend a lot of time laughing together

makes them both feel good. The clitoris is more sensitive than a penis, and many girls don't like it touched or rubbed until they are quite excited—some not even then. Boys like to be touched in many different ways and many different places. Good lovers go exploring together. They also talk, and tell what they like and don't like.

FANTASIES

Many if not most people have sexual daydreams ("fantasies") especially when they masturbate, but also at other times. These can simply be about having sex with someone attractive (someone you know, a movie star) or they can be quite wild—film scripts, like being Pharaoh or a prostitute or a Roman emperor; things you wouldn't in fact ever do, or even things you wouldn't enjoy if they really happened, like being raped. The fantasies of "straight" people are quite often about homosexual play.

All this is perfectly normal.

Fantasies are a part of the play-function of sex, so if you have them, enjoy them to the full, however wild they are. By contrast some people never or hardly ever have sexual fantasies. That is perfectly normal too. Fantasies are like dreams, but being awake one can write the script for them, which makes them a very good experience for people who have them. The people who don't are often those who concentrate on good bodily feelings in sex, rather than exciting ideas. Both are good ways of enjoying sex as play.

SEX ROLES

Our sex is fixed originally by whether we have XX or XY chromosomes in our cells, and our shape and the kind of sex organs we have depend upon whether we have male or female sex hormones. How we behave is *learned*, and learning starts early. In fact, when a child who is really a boy is brought up as a girl, he'll behave like a girl, or vice versa.

Ideas that men and women should behave quite differently might have had uses in the past, but now they can make for trouble by not letting us be our real selves. Girls were once supposed to be quiet, gentle, not interested in machinery, interested in cooking and babies, and destined to get married, have babies and wait on men. *Some* girls might like to be like this. Others wouldn't, but they are not given the choice. Boys were supposed to be brave, manly, fond of rough games, and never to show any emotion like fear or gentleness. *Some* boys are like this. Others wouldn't be if it weren't laid on them. This kind of training starts very early. When people were shown a baby dressed as a boy, they gave it toy ships or bricks—when the same baby was dressed as a girl, they gave it dolls. If you look at children's books, they often still show boys doing all the active things and girls watching them.

In fact, the only thing a woman can't possibly do is father a baby, and the only thing a man can't possibly do is bear one or suckle one. The idea of manhood and womanhood has varied wildly from one time and place to another. At one time women were expected to be scared of mice and scream if they saw blood, because that was "womanly." At another they were expected to be guerrillas or land with airborne troops, and that was womanly too.

Girls have suffered most from this because men have stopped them from taking jobs which they are perfectly able to do, in business and elsewhere. There are women doctors now, and women who are civil airline pilots. But men have often treated them, when they did get jobs like those of men, as people to joke at and try to have sex with rather than as colleagues. Women have had to fight against this sort of nonsense and are still doing so. It's much less than 100 years since men let them vote. But men have suffered too. They had to be studs, heroes and tough guys who didn't allow themselves any feelings, couldn't cry if they were unhappy, and had to act like John Wayne's portrayal of a cowboy.

We're only just beginning to get out from under this nonsense, and both sexes will be happier when we do. So long as people think

Women have been supposed to be "feminine"...

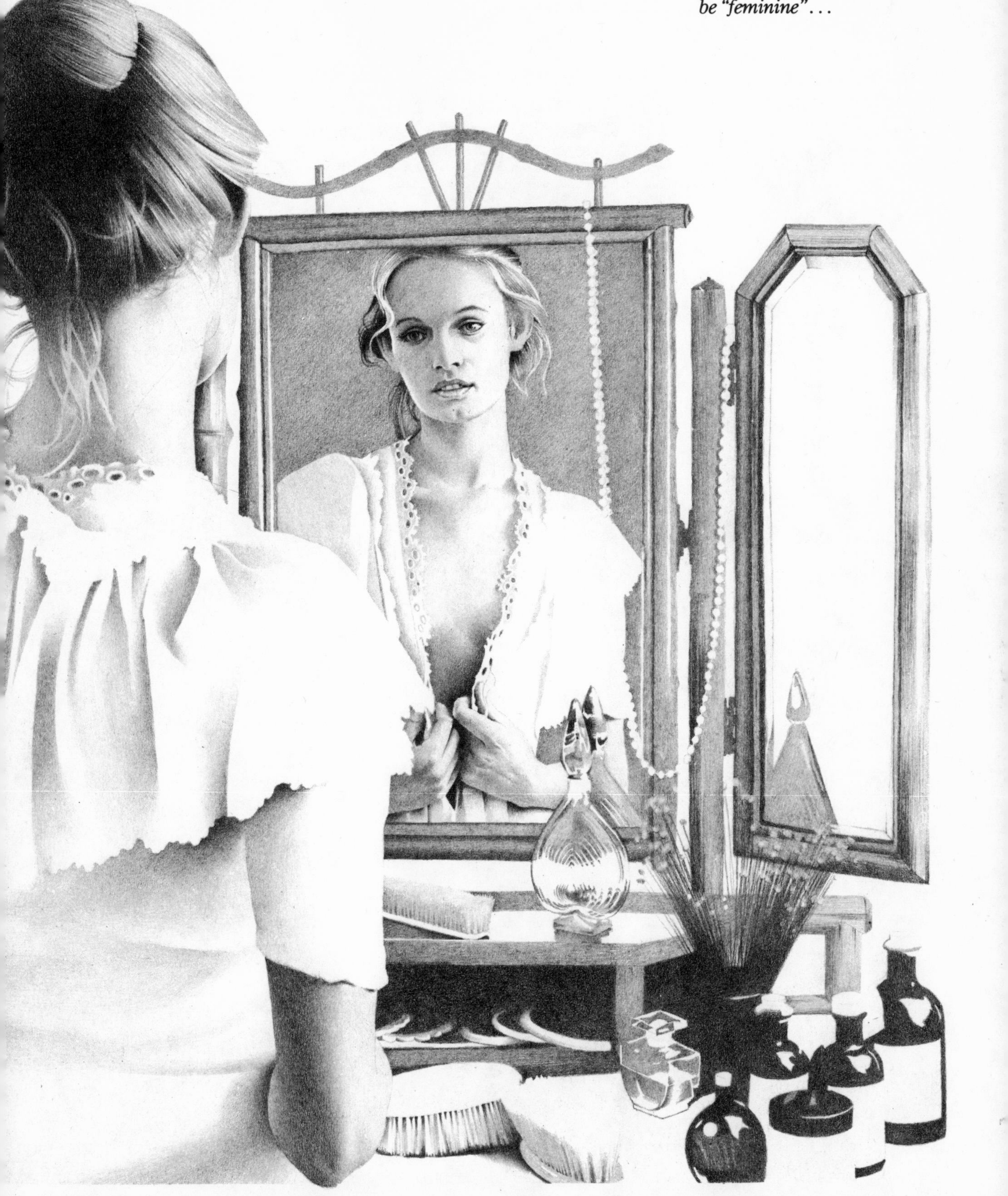

106 *. . . and men to be "tough."*
Many of these preconceived
ideas about men and women
have been acted for us by
movie stars

that women are weak or emotional and that men have to act like prize bulls, both sexes suffer.

To enjoy the sex you are, you have to realize that men and women are equals. They can do the same things if they choose and different things if they choose. Neither sex is smarter, better, more intelligent, more emotional than the other, and neither has the right to be boss and call the shots for the other. Both sexes are people and all people are different. What every man and every woman has to find out is what sort of person he or she is, and what he or she needs in life. Often, then, a man and a woman who really care about and respect each other can help each other do just this.

It's good for a girl to want to be "feminine"—if that means, proud of being a woman and proud of having a female body. It's not so good if she thinks "feminine" means born to get married as soon as she can lay hands on a man, and then destined to wait on him, do dishes and have babies. There's nothing bad about doing dishes, or looking after babies—sensible men and women if they do marry, take turns doing these, though they can't physically take turns actually *having* babies. The point is that they aren't "women's work" any more or less than they are men's work, nor is a woman incomplete if she chooses not to marry at all. It's good for a boy to be manly, if that means proud of being a man and willing to tackle any job which he can tackle. It's not so good if it makes him think it's sissy to be gentle and have feelings, or to take his share of work at home, or if it makes him angry and jealous if he sees a woman doing the same work that he does, and maybe doing it better. When men act this way it's not because they are very masculine but because they are very uncertain inside. Men who play very tough, who put down women and treat them as inferior, and who behave like bad imitations of a stage cowboy usually have inside them a very small man who isn't really sure *how* male he is. Often their trouble is that they are so scared of women that they have quite a lot of trouble in functioning sexually. People who have this kind of trouble can be helped a lot by talking with a skilled counselor. The first thing they have to learn then is to get a truer idea of what being male is really about.

Girls have not had quite this trip laid on them. They have suffered more from being put down by insecure men. But they too need to resist pressures from men and from women who tell them what is or isn't "feminine" without asking them what kind of "feminine" they themselves want to be. It's feminine to be a home-maker, and it's equally feminine to have a career, to be president of a corporation, to choose to marry, to choose not to marry—in fact, to be *themselves*. It's also feminine to stand up for their right to choose among all of these for themselves, and the right of other women to choose. Men and women will get on best with one another, and have the biggest range of choice, when they stop trying to impose set roles on each other and realize that all people—male and female—are people, and all are different. Then all people can be fully male or fully female—in their own different ways.

You will sometimes hear people talk about being "macho," and taking it to mean "being a male tough guy who behaves like an oaf toward women." Macho is the Spanish for "male, masculine." In Mexico, where sex roles are still often very much separated, with men going out to work and women staying home, "machismo" means "being man enough to provide for all the children you produce." Even in our culture, where both man and woman often work to provide for children, it's not such a bad attitude for either parent.

INNER DIRECTION

People who know where they are going and make their own choices are called "inner-directed" people—which means that they make up their own minds. If Abraham Lincoln or Joan of Arc or Albert Schweitzer had started by figuring out what would be popular with other people and doing that, we probably would never have heard of them.

This doesn't mean you have to pretend you are holier than your friends—they have a right to choose too. But make your own choices, even if you "lose friends." Friends who won't let you say "No, thank you, I don't choose to" aren't much worth having as friends. Often they are quite glad inside to see someone who makes up his or her mind and doesn't just go with the gang.

MARRIAGE

If you ask boys or girls what they hope to do in life, they will mention careers—being a pilot, a doctor, a farmer, a dancer—doing particular things, such as traveling or being famous. Often one thing they will mention is getting married and having a family.

Not all the jobs one would like to do when one is young turn out to be things one can do when one is older. Having a family, if one wants that, has been something which everyone reckons to be able to do, and in fact many people will get married, and many of those will want to raise children.

Here are some facts about marriage and about having a family that are real. First of all, marriage isn't compulsory—some people, who realize that being married involves giving time to another person, taking responsibility and caring, reckon that there are other things they want to do in life. Since they feel they can't do two jobs properly—still less three, if you include bringing up children—they choose a career instead.

Second, marriage is intended to last. You don't want to undertake it with someone you can't happily spend your life with. Many marriages now end in divorce, but that was not what the parties intended to happen. One very wise and happy married couple, were asked if they'd ever thought of divorce. The wife jokingly said "Divorce never—murder frequently!" Evidently their love had so much give and take that they didn't divorce or stop loving each other.

Third, beside being about love and sex, marriage is about a great many other things, including money, one or both people's careers, finding a house, paying bills. You have to be ready to deal with all these other things, beside caring for each other and liking to be together.

Fourth, the pressure is on to hurry. Just as you should not rush into sex until you are ready, so you should not think that you can solve problems or score points by getting married before you know your own mind. Two loving people can be happy together and make each other happy, but they need to know their own minds and one another. They need to take their time, to finish their training, to see where they are going. And they cannot be giver-uppers who quarrel and part at the first difficulty. It is a fact that very early marriages more often end in divorce. Some of these will happen because the girl became pregnant and married for that reason. Sometimes young people will deliberately start a pregnancy so that elders will have to let them marry. At other times young people will have a great relationship with each other and will have insisted on marrying too young. They may not realize how much people change between 16 and 25, or how much easier it is to love and avoid problems when both of them live at home and only meet for the good times they have together. Many people do marry happily with a first love. But even so it is better to take a little longer over choosing.

Having a family, too, is something you should choose and understand before you choose. Young people often love babies and think they are cute. So they are, but they are there all day and all night. They need diapers changed, they need comforting at night, they can stop you going out, or studying, or working at something else. They are also lovable. Youngsters, however, who think of them as dolls or toys or pets usually haven't been around real babies. That is why, even when you are married, babies shouldn't just happen.

110 *Doctors and professional counselors can help on specific questions. The Yellow Pages usually contain a list of professional advisers you can contact in confidence*

GETTING HELP

Sex is no different from other good things in life—it sometimes produces problems. Some of these can be avoided by knowing the facts: others happen because of mistakes we or other people make. We have to talk about problems as well as all the pleasant things which sex brings. It would be silly to pretend they don't exist.

People who do have a problem in their sexual behavior often feel very alone, especially if they are young. It can be something other people will understand—like being upset because someone we like doesn't like us. But often it is something we feel we can't easily talk about. The young boy or girl who thinks he or she may have caught an infection from a sex partner, the girl who is afraid that she may be pregnant, the youngster who has had a frightening or an unpleasant sex experience, all have this in common—they don't want other people to know, and they don't know quite what to do.

LEARNING TO GET HELP IF EVER YOU ARE IN TROUBLE IS VERY, VERY IMPORTANT. Problems we have with our feelings won't go away if you say nothing about them: venereal disease or pregnancy don't go away either. In any of these situations, people need help.

There are two ways to get help, and two kinds of people who can give it. The first kind are adults you really trust, and for most people the adults they ought to be able to talk with are their parents. If something really serious has happened, they have to know about it, and the sooner you talk to them the better. The other kind are experts of various kinds. If you catch an illness, you have to see a doctor. If you are in trouble and don't know quite what to do, there are health professionals, clergy, school counselors. Pick someone you like, if you can, and someone you can talk to frankly. DON'T KEEP PROBLEMS TO YOURSELF. Friends of your own age can help a little if they are sensible, and often they are the first people that youngsters trust with their problems, but if those friends are really sensible they will tell you to get adult help as soon as you can. If you are sensible and friends bring bad problems to you, you'll listen to them carefully, then tell them to get adult help. All the problems people have with sexuality are made much worse if they are afraid to talk about them. Help is there if you need it. Usually you will find that parents and professionals understand your feelings, and it's a great relief when they do. Parents, incidentally, aren't only there to be talked to when you're in trouble. If you talk to them at other times you can learn a lot, avoid trouble and they'll be around when you need them.

ALCOHOL & OTHER DRUGS

Alcohol is something we have to learn to live with in our society, because you are sure to be offered it, and many people drink it. We put it in here because a lot of sexual accidents happen when people have been drinking. Alcohol is not a "stimulant"—it is, in fact, a downer, which interferes with the working of the brain, but the sensation which this produces makes anxious people feel relaxed and sociable.

You might not realize it from society's attitude, but alcohol is actually the most dangerous drug of addiction in modern society. Other, illegal, drugs are also very dangerous, but this one is legal, and everybody pushes it. The reason it isn't called a "dangerous drug," like heroin or cocaine, is that laws are made by people who use alcohol, not heroin or cocaine. About one person in nine who drinks at all will develop a serious addiction problem, but even if one isn't addicted and doesn't get obviously drunk, small amounts of alcohol upset the ability to drive a car, take careful contraceptive precautions, and generally behave at full attention. They can also affect judgment and involve you in sex situations you wouldn't normally have accepted. More than half of all road accidents are partly due to someone drinking. In the years of the Vietnam war, about 45,000 American soldiers were killed by bullets and bombs. In the same years, 274,000 Americans died in motor accidents due largely or wholly to alcohol, and it is estimated that it plays a part in about 70 percent of murders. It seems, however, to be here to stay. The attempt 50 years ago to make it an illegal drug ("Prohibition") was a failure and probably did more harm than good.

There are two strategies in dealing with alcohol. Some people try to "drink sensibly"—that is to say, to know exactly how much they are drinking, and never drink enough to alter their brain function much. This is not always easy—it is particularly hard with mixed drinks served cold and containing fruit juice (punches, vodka and orange, mai-tais, margaritas) because these can range from lemonade to a knockout depending on who mixes them, and one cannot taste how strong they are. A normal-sized adult can burn up the alcohol in a twelve-ounce bottle of beer, a biggish wineglass of wine, or a shot-and-a-half of hard liquor (whisky, gin, vodka) every hour without having brain function much upset. After that a lot depends on the people, on how big they are, on whether they drink with or without eating, and on what the alcohol is mixed with. Fizzy mixtures (champagne, whisky and soda) are absorbed faster and more likely to make you drunk with the same amount of alcohol than still drinks like wine. Many people still think it funny to put spirit into other folk's drinks in order to make them "happy" or "sociable," and girls in particular need to watch for jokers who get them drunk in order to have sex with them.

Alcohol is a top cause of unwanted pregnancy.

People who manage to handle alcohol without trouble are usually the fortunate group who actively dislike the sensation caused by having too much of it. If you like that sensation, and find it makes you feel big, relaxed and able to deal with people and problems when normally you aren't, it is a risky drug to take. Quite small amounts also reduce some people's ability to exercise common sense and stop drinking, and there is no way of knowing in advance if you are one of the ten percent whose chemistry, problems, or both, make them likely to be addicted. Alcoholic addiction is now recognized as a disease, not a vice or a bad habit. It can be treated at any time, but it takes an average of fifteen years before most addicted people recognize their problem and come for treatment, by which time they are in bad trouble.

The other strategy, obviously, is simply not to drink the stuff. About one American in four has adopted this approach: if you ever have problems with alcohol, it is the only one you can adopt. Some young people are inclined to "go along" with drinking, as they may run risks with other drugs, if their friends do. If you decide to adopt the nondrinking strategy, you can deal with people who think you ought to drink by telling them you prefer your head straight—and with people who think you ought to offer them drinks by saying that you prefer your friends with *their* heads straight. If the people you mix with won't accept this, you need to change your friends. People who have no alcohol problem often make it harder for people who have by bringing out "drinks" as a feature of every social gathering, and you can't tell among your friends who the folk with problems are. The typical alcoholic isn't a Skid Row bum but a respectable suburban man or woman who may not realize the trouble they are in, and nor may you.

These are the basic facts, and the choice is yours, but one absolute rule could well be never to drive a car, and, while you have to avoid pregnancy, never to have sexual relations, if you've been drinking *at all*. Married girls who want children should also know that heavy drinking, even on one occasion during early pregnancy, can permanently damage the baby. This has only recently been shown to be so, and one can't be sure that even small amounts of alcohol taken by a pregnant woman don't do some damage. If you do drink and find that you can't stop or do without it, get help at once: alcohol counseling services are listed in the Yellow Pages.

It's worth knowing that quite small amounts of alcohol can prevent some males from getting an erection: in fact, taking a drink under the impression that it boosts sexual feeling or performance is quite a common cause of impotency. Many males don't know this.

Alcohol is dangerous because it is legal and people pretend it is harmless. You know by now that illegal drugs are dangerous. Anything you take "to feel good" is a bad idea, because unless you are ill and need medicine you should be able to feel good about yourself as a matter of course. Some illegal drugs, and some silly tricks like glue-sniffing, are killers. Others, like smoking pot, are illegal rather than very harmful. The real reason for avoiding them, apart from not breaking the law, is that to be at your best as a person you need your head straight. You need it straight to drive a car, to work well, to have good sex, and to be able to act in a caring way toward other people.

Doctors see hundreds of kids every year who experiment with drugs and really mess up their lives. The fact that some kids boast that they use drugs and are none the worse proves nothing. They may be just boasting, or in more trouble than they realize, and drugs might still kill you. So don't run the risk.

There must be something wrong with a person who wants to be confused, stoned or "high." Some people experiment with illegal drugs out of curiosity or because other people do. It pays to remember that there are many drugs around now on the street and in schools that can harm you seriously with only a single dose. The sensible thing is to stay away from all of them—pills, things you sniff, injections, the lot. Incidentally there is no known drug (or medicine) which can "turn a person on" sexually—not even sex hormones work like this regardless.

Drinking alcohol, taking drugs, having sex, wearing long hair, listening to a particular sort of music, using particular words, are all examples of things which people often do, or don't do, not because they have thought out what they want or really enjoy and what is sensible for them, but because other people, especially people their own age, do or don't do them, and they want to be popular. All people often feel that to be liked they have to do as others do. In the short run this can be true, but when the thing in question is harmful, or illegal, or not what you personally would choose, the short run isn't worth it. This can be true of sex—a lot of young people try it before they are ready for it or comfortable with it in order to "go along" with what other young people *say* they do.

DISEASES

You can catch flu or measles from a sexual partner, just as you can from a dancing partner. There are some diseases which one can only catch by having sex with a person who has them. These are called venereal diseases. They are getting commoner because people are having sex with more people than they did, and because very little has been done to tell young folk how to avoid or prevent getting infected. Some "moral" people have always had the idea that the risk of catching an illness would help to frighten others into acting in the way the moralists thought right and staying away from sex. Because of this idea it has been hard to treat venereal diseases just like other diseases. Often people who catch them have been afraid or ashamed to get quick treatment. This is a pity, because the diseases are easily cured if you treat them when they start, but can cause a lot of harm if you let them go untreated.

The most common venereal diseases are called gonorrhea ("clap") and syphilis ("pox"). Gonorrhea is an infection of the urine pipe and of the vagina and lubricating glands. Actually, there are two diseases—gonorrhea and chlamydial urethritis, which only tests can tell apart. In boys they start with pain in the tip of the penis, stinging when urine is passed, and a yellow or white discharge. They usually hurt quite a lot. If they are not treated they appear to go away, but they may hang around and do harm to the boy's waterworks and injure his ability to father children, beside causing other illnesses. In girls there may be stinging and a discharge, and soreness of the lips of the vulva. Girls quite often get soreness and discharge from other causes, so they may not know they have the disease, but it can hurt their ability to have babies and it can do other damage. Gonorrhea is quite easily cured by one or two injections, but this has to be done by a doctor who can check that it has really gone. It usually takes three to five days after infection for gonorrhea to show, but it can take as long as a month.

Syphilis starts in both sexes as a hard, painless pimple on the penis or the lips of the vulva or anywhere else around the genitals or mouth where the germs have entered a tiny wound—even on the finger. This pimple appears from ten to 90 days after infection— usually three weeks. The pimple turns into a hard-edged ulcer, looking like a crater on the moon, and about half an inch across or less, which still doesn't hurt. After a time this heals up and goes away, but the infected person may start to get skin rashes, pains, and sore places in the mouth and vagina and at this stage the disease is very catching—even by kissing. Fortunately even in women the pimple that marks the start of the illness is usually near the outside where one can see it or feel it.

Syphilis is a really dangerous disease which can last for years and damage the heart or the brain—it is also one of the few diseases which can be passed on to an unborn baby. Luckily it is even easier to cure than gonorrhea if you go to the doctor early, before harm has been done.

The only way you can get these illnesses is by having sex, or intimate sex play like kissing, with someone who has them and has not been treated. You can't catch them from bath water or toilet seats. Venereal diseases are one of the things which spoil the pleasure and freedom of sex, and you need to watch for them—in yourself, so they can be treated, and in your partner. Never have sex with anyone who has a discharge from the genitals, or sores, or a lot of redness and soreness, and never have sex yourself with anyone if you find you have these, but see a doctor or go to a free clinic. Not all discharges or sore places mean gonorrhea or syphilis, but there are other minor infections that are catching too, so stick to this rule. Unless you know each other well, and know that neither of you ever has sex with other people, it is a good idea after having sex for the boy to pass urine and lather his penis all over with soapsuds, right up to the root. The girl should pass urine and wash her vulva very thoroughly with soap lather. Don't use "deodorant" soap, as this can make you sore by itself. Using a sheath gives quite a lot of protection from venereal diseases, but you should still wash. The Pill actually makes the girl a bit more likely to catch things—not only these, but some tiresome things called yeasts and trichomonads, which make her itch and produce a nasty-smelling discharge ("whites"). These aren't venereal diseases but can be passed around. The reason is that the Pill turns off some of the natural acid in her secretions which is there to kill germs.

Most women get some irritation or discharge at some time in their lives—often this is due to washing with deodorant soap, wearing all-nylon panties, or using some of the sprays, douches and so on which people are trying to sell them. If you have any discomfort you should get advice.

Obviously if somebody has sex with a great many people he or she is more likely to catch something, just as kissing everyone makes you more likely to catch flu. On the other hand, the next worst thing to having a venereal disease is being so scared you will catch one that you become terrified of ever having sex—this is much harder to deal with than the diseases themselves would be if you caught them.

Sensible people try to avoid catching disease by being careful whom they have sex with. They wash carefully after sex if they ever have it with someone they don't know well, keep a maintenance check on themselves and go without fear to a doctor or clinic if they think anything is wrong. They also tell their partner at once if trouble starts, and never risk somebody else's health by having sex with them if they think something *may* be wrong. It's not very friendly to have sex with someone if you have a bad cold or any other catching disease, even if it's not "venereal." If we could treat venereal diseases like any other disease—as an illness not a moral problem—we could get rid of them in your lifetime.

PORNOGRAPHY

One of the troubles about treating sex as something dangerous and prohibited has been that people were both excited about it and guilty at wanting it. When something is forbidden, it can be sold, like liquor during Prohibition, or drugs today. You can see the results of this in all big cities, where there are people selling "sex" as a commodity—adult book stores, sex magazines, massage parlors where one can pay to have sex of a kind. If people really got loving enjoyment out of this kind of thing it might not matter, but what it really means is anxiety. If people weren't anxious, and were enjoying sex the way it can be between two people who have no fears about it and nothing to sell, this whole scene would go out of business. Many men in particular who go to these places are worried that they cannot "perform" sexually. As long as they think of sex as a performance, rather than something which happens when you are ready for it, they will go on "not performing." Sex between caring people is quite different, even if it is no more than play.

Pornography is a long word for any kind of book or movie about sex which somebody wants to prohibit. Most people who like football, like looking at pictures of football and reading books about football. Since nearly every normal person enjoys sex, nearly every normal person might well enjoy reading about it or seeing pictures of it, if anxious folk didn't prevent them. There are plenty of books with pictures of naked people or of people having sex, and many people quite enjoy looking at these. The only trouble is that pictures can't show what the people are feeling about each other, and this, rather than just intercourse only, is one of the things sex is about.

These pictures are quite useful in making us used to seeing what naked men and women are like, and to the naturalness of all the different ways people enjoy sex. Some are devoted to dressing-up, or to rather rough sexual games. The idea of these excites some people, though one might not necessarily want to copy them. Others show actual cruelty, and appeal to people who confuse the energetic side of lovemaking with actually hurting someone. If children see two adults making love, and making a lot of noise about it, they often mistake it for fighting. Others are homosexual pictures, and appeal to people who prefer to make love to people of their own sex.

Reading pornography won't hurt you, though you probably won't learn very much from it, and it often contains a lot of exaggerated or anxious ideas about sex. Some adults flip if they see children with this kind of reading matter. If the children have been taught the facts about sex, these adults really need not worry. What you don't learn from pornography is how to treat other people in sexual matters, and that is the most important lesson. A lot of boys, and grown men too, like to have pictures of naked girls to look at when they masturbate. There's nothing wrong with this. It enables them to imagine sexual things which would please or excite them and can make masturbation more fun. Many people like to have fantasies of this sort—they are one of the pleasant things about sex which you can enjoy even when you are alone.

People used to say that girls don't enjoy sex pictures as much as boys. Maybe this was because they used to be taught that it wasn't ladylike to look at such things. At any rate a lot of women's magazines have spreads now of naked men, just as men's magazines have pictures of naked women. Since men and women are programmed to find each others' bodies exciting (and there would be no people if they didn't) there doesn't seem anything wrong with this.

Probably the real trouble with sex pictures is that all the girls are photographic models and all the boys are muscle men, and most of us aren't either of these. In magazine pictures, all the pimples are taken out with an air brush. These people belong to an unreal world. Real sex is for ordinary people like us.

RAPE

Rape means forcing someone to have sex with you when that person doesn't want it—either by real force or by frightening the victim into giving in. Since men are usually stronger than women, this is something women have to be concerned about. No boy or man *ever* has the right to force a woman to have sex with him, even if he is very excited, and even if she changes her mind and says "No" after saying "Yes." But this is not usually why rape happens. Men who rape women are not "very sexual" or "easily excited"—they are people who use sex to express hate, not love. Raping a woman, like beating her, is simply a way of giving her pain and distress.

Unfortunately, there must be a lot of people now who are full of hate, because rape often happens, and girls and women have to learn to protect themselves—by not going about alone at night, by not hitch-hiking or taking rides from strangers, by carrying a whistle to call for help. This is sad, but you have to know about it, because it is true. It's not true that if a girl or woman is attacked, it shows that she asked for it, by wearing sexy clothes or in some other way. Old ladies are attacked as well as young girls. Rape is a terribly frightening thing if it happens, but it is important that any woman to whom it does happen should tell the police, and any young girl to whom it happens should tell her parents—not only because there is a risk she might have a baby, but also because the person who raped her might do the same to other people. People who have had this experience need help and advice anyway. Of course you do not need to be scared of being raped all the time, but if you know about it, you can avoid running risks. Taking a big dog around with you when you walk, or jog, or cycle alone is one way of keeping out of trouble.

If you are a boy, by the way, the law is that having sex with someone who is under the legal age for your state, even if she is willing, is also called rape, and you can go to jail for it.

SEX IS...

So there is a lot more to sex than the mere fact that people are male or female, or the way that babies are born. It means the attraction that human beings feel for one another, the physical ways they express that attraction, the use of man–woman relationships to express love, to express playfulness, or to produce children. It covers all the different needs that people have, their beliefs about what is right or wrong, and the way they see themselves as men or as women. There are rules which have to be followed if the sexual experience is to be a good and happy one—not treating other people selfishly and uncaringly, not producing an unwanted child because we are careless or excited or didn't believe it could happen to us. It covers some dangers we need to know about so that we can avoid them.

There is a lot to learn. Some of the facts—how exactly babies are made, how they come to be male or female, what happens when a baby is born—are fascinating in themselves, apart from our need to know how our bodies work. We can get this kind of factual knowledge from diagrams and films.

How sexuality *feels*, what it is like to be in love with another

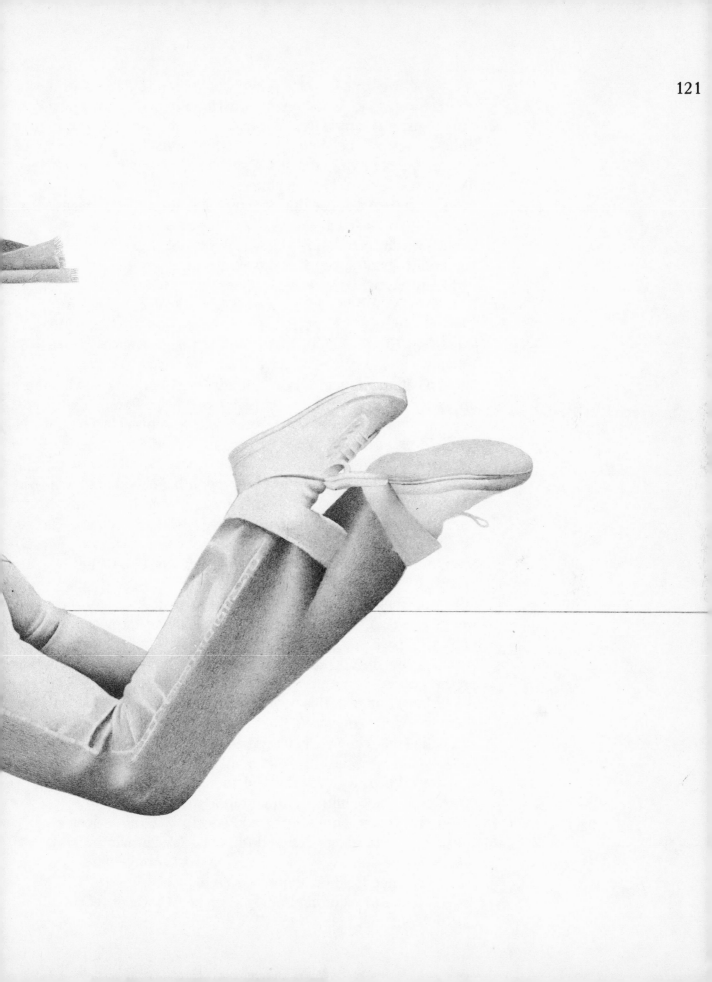

person, why adults feel so strongly about their sex lives—even why people have found sexual relations frightening or difficult to handle—can't really be learned from books, though one can learn *about* these things. They only become real when they actually happen to us. One can read *about* flying in a space ship—to know what it really feels like one has to do it. The big difference is that sex is something which most people experience during their lives. It can be just as much an adventure: it makes just as big demands on us. If you knew that you would one day crew on Skylab you'd probably learn just as much as you could about space travel well ahead of time, not wait until it suddenly happened and then wonder why you ran risks and got into trouble. KNOWING ENOUGH TO ENJOY A VERY BIG ADVENTURE AND NOT SPOIL IT FOR YOURSELF OR FOR OTHER PEOPLE IS WHAT THIS BOOK IS REALLY ABOUT. When we do fall in love, or have to make a choice in sexual matters, or even get into difficulties over them, we are not on our own—there are people we can turn to for advice and help. Parents, who have been around longer than you have, and who brought you into the world, are there to be talked to; even if you and they sometimes find this kind of talking difficult, it helps to remember that growing up is something which happens to everyone; it happened to parents too.

It's much easier to give advice to someone who wants to be a climber or an astronaut than to someone who is growing up. The best advice—which would apply to climbing or space travel too—is probably this: don't be in too much of a hurry, don't start until you are ready and know what you are doing, don't be scared, and ask for advice from someone you trust if you don't know what to do, or if things don't go according to plan. You can get the facts from this book: what we can't give you is experience. That comes with time and growing up. You can't make a young tree grow faster by pulling on the leaves.

Where things in this book are specially important, we have put them in several times. We think you have got the main rules which you will need to know when you become, and *as* you become, sexual adults—but here they are, one more time:

—don't be in a hurry. Sexual intercourse is for men and women, not children, and there is *plenty of time*.
—do be considerate, caring and sensitive to other people's needs and feelings. Never do other people harm in any way.
—don't ever, on any account, run the risk of producing a baby whose needs you will not be able to meet.
—do learn to value and enjoy your body without fear, but without ever being selfish.

SO...

If you read this book carefully, you now know most of the important things about sex in humans—except, of course, how it feels, and how close a man and a woman can come to one another through using it in a caring way. At the very least you know—because we said it several times—that you have to use it in a caring way, and that this includes caring about the fact that sex can produce a baby. A baby is a new person who needs to be cared for too, and you must never risk producing one that you can't or won't care for simply because sex feels good and you get excited wanting it.

We don't know, of course, just how old you are. If you are young and just getting to puberty, you can enjoy reading this book now, but you will probably need to keep coming back to it as you get older. If you are already older, and have reached the time when sexual feelings and needs are getting important, at least you will know the facts and will not be ready to believe nonsense.

All sensible people control their sex behavior and use it with responsibility and good manners. It is easier to do this if you know what the guidelines are and why they are there, rather than because people have preached at you or tried to scare you. In the long run, you are the person who has to choose what you will do and how you will do it. All we have done here is to give you some facts and tips, so that what you choose to do is sensible and rewarding, both for you and for other people with whom you share your sexuality.

Index

Index

Index

Acknowledgements

The illustrations on pages 6-7, 24, 26-7, 32, 34, 35, 36, 37, 38-9, 41, 44-5, 46-7, 48, 49, 51, 53, 65, 68-9, 70, 71, 72, 88, 90-91, 92-3, 105, 106, 120-121 are by Howard Pemberton;
those on pages 20-21, 22-3, 28, 58-9, 60-61, 62-3, 74-5, 77, 82-3, 84-5, 102-103, 110 are by Bill Prosser;
and those on pages 18-19, 30-31, 97, 100-101 are by Rod Ferring.

Diagrams by Hayward & Martin Ltd.

The publishers would like to thank Kim Sayer, Maggi Heinz and Shevanthi de Silva.